CGP
–books
like no others!

CGP

Reading Shakespeare can be a real headache

That's why we've put this book together.

We've put notes handily next to the play so you don't have to go hunting for
"Note 136". That means you can understand what all the weird bits mean
without losing the flow of the play.

We've written the notes in plain English to make it just that bit easier.

There's even the odd bit of ever-so-nearly entertaining humour in the
notes and pictures to help you breeze through the toughest of scenes.

We've done our bit — the rest is up to you.

What CGP is all about

Our sole aim here at CGP is to produce the highest quality
books — carefully written, immaculately presented and
dangerously close to being funny.

Then we work our socks off to get them out to you
— at the cheapest possible prices.

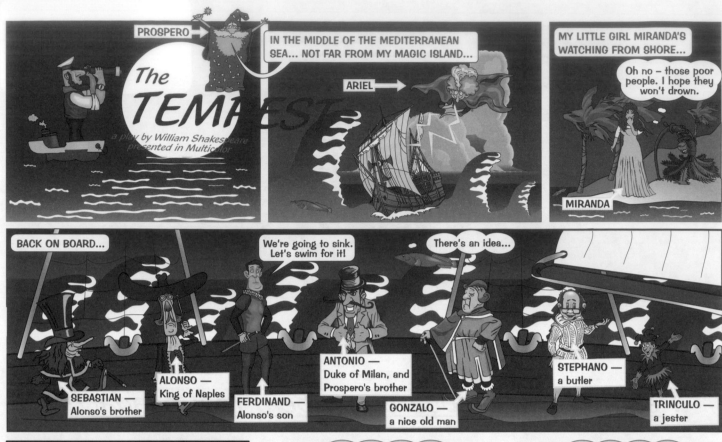

PROSPERO

The TEMPEST
a play by William Shakespeare
presented in Multicolor

IN THE MIDDLE OF THE MEDITERRANEAN SEA... NOT FAR FROM MY MAGIC ISLAND...

ARIEL

MY LITTLE GIRL MIRANDA'S WATCHING FROM SHORE...

Oh no – those poor people. I hope they won't drown.

MIRANDA

BACK ON BOARD...

We're going to sink. Let's swim for it!

There's an idea...

SEBASTIAN — Alonso's brother

ALONSO — King of Naples

FERDINAND — Alonso's son

ANTONIO — Duke of Milan, and Prospero's brother

GONZALO — a nice old man

STEPHANO — a butler

TRINCULO — a jester

MIRANDA COMES TO SEE ME AT THE BEACH HUT...

Did you start this storm, dad?

Yes – and I'll tell you why. It all started many years ago...

Believe it or not I used to be Duke of Milan, but I was into books and magic, not politics...

ALONSO

ANTONIO

My brother Antonio and the scheming King of Naples hatched a plot to get rid of me...

They threw you and me out of Milan and set us adrift on the open sea in a leaky old boat... Luckily, good old Gonzalo put my books of magic on the boat.

It's pure chance we didn't drown. We ended up on this island.

There was nobody here, apart from that idiot-monster Caliban...

...good old Ariel...

...and a load of other magical spirits.

So now do you see why I started the storm? All my enemies are on that ship. They won't drown but I'm going to teach them a lesson.

CONTENTS

Act 1

Scene 1 1

Alonso, the King of Naples, has just been to Tunis, for his daughter's wedding. He's sailing back to Naples with his son Ferdinand, his brother Sebastian, an advisor called Gonzalo and Antonio, the Duke of Milan, when a terrible storm hits the ship. It looks like the ship's going to sink so they decide to jump off and swim for it.

Scene 2 3

On an island nearby, a young woman called Miranda is watching the storm. She's worried about the people on the ship. Her dad, Prospero, tells her the story of how they both ended up living on the island — he used to be Duke of Milan but his brother Antonio kicked him out with Alonso's help. Prospero's arranged the storm to bring Alonso and Antonio to the island. He sends his spirit-helper Ariel to fetch Ferdinand. Prospero's deformed slave, Caliban, enters and argues with Prospero and Miranda before Prospero sends him off to work. As soon as Miranda sees Ferdinand, she falls in love with him. Prospero pretends to think Ferdinand's a spy to test Miranda's feelings and Ferdinand's honesty.

Revision Summary 16

Act 2

Scene 1 17

Alonso, Antonio, Sebastian and Gonzalo have ended up on a different part of the island from Ferdinand. Alonso and Gonzalo are worn out so Antonio and Sebastian offer to keep watch while they sleep. Antonio persuades Sebastian to kill Alonso so that Sebastian can be King of Naples, but Ariel wakes Gonzalo up just in time to stop their plot.

Scene 2 25

The jester, Trinculo, has been washed up on a third part of the island. He finds Caliban lying on the ground and decides to crawl under his coat to shelter from the rain. Alonso's butler, Stephano, finds them there and shares out some wine he saved from the ship. Caliban loves the wine and offers to be Stephano's servant, believing him to be a god.

Revision Summary 29

Act 3

Scene 1 30
Miranda feels sorry for Ferdinand — Prospero has made him a prisoner and ordered him to shift piles of heavy logs. Ferdinand doesn't mind as long as he can see and talk to Miranda.

Scene 2 33
Caliban, Stephano and Trinculo are all really drunk. Caliban persuades Stephano to kill Prospero and make himself king of the island.

Scene 3 36
Alonso, Gonzalo, Sebastian and Antonio have been looking for Ferdinand. They stop for a break and some of Prospero's spirits bring in a feast. They're just about to eat it when Ariel comes in and makes the feast vanish. Ariel tells them the shipwreck was their punishment for throwing Prospero out of Milan.

Revision Summary 40

Act 4

Scene 1 41
Prospero admits he wasn't really cross with Ferdinand, just testing, and says it's fine if he wants to marry Miranda. He uses his magical spirits to put on a special entertainment for the happy couple. Then Prospero suddenly remembers that Caliban, Stephano and Trinculo are on their way to kill him and he breaks off the show.

Revision Summary 48

Act 5

Scene 1 49
Ariel brings Alonso and the other nobles to Prospero. He casts a final spell on them and reminds them of their past crimes, but then he forgives them. He reveals that Ferdinand is still alive and is going to marry Miranda. Stephano, Trinculo and Caliban get a ticking off too and are sent to tidy Prospero's home for the visitors. Finally, Prospero tells Ariel he's free to go — once Ariel arranges good weather for the return trip to Italy.

Epilogue 57
Prospero speaks directly to the audience — he asks for them to help him on his journey home.

Revision Summary 58

Published by CGP

Editors:
Taissa Csáky
Charley Darbishire
John Kitching
Tim Major
Katherine Reed
Ed Robinson
Emma Stevens
Jennifer Underwood

ISBN: 978 1 84146 530 2

With thanks to Ed Robinson, Keri Barrow and Paula Barnett for the proofreading.

Clipart from Corel®

Printed by Elanders Ltd, Newcastle upon Tyne.

Based on the classic CGP style created by Richard Parsons.

0800 1712 712 · www.cgpbooks.co.uk

ACT 1 SCENE 1
On a ship at sea

> Antonio, Alonso, Ferdinand, Sebastian and Gonzalo are on board a ship in a terrible storm. The sailors work hard to save the ship but it looks like they're all going to drown.

A tempestuous noise of thunder and lightning is heard.
Enter a SHIPMASTER and a BOATSWAIN.

MASTER Boatswain!

BOATSWAIN Here, master. What cheer?

> *boatswain = second-in-command on ship. Pronounced 'bo-sun'.*

> *2 'What's going on?'*

MASTER Good! Speak to th' mariners. Fall to't yarely, or we run ourselves aground. Bestir, bestir!

> *3-4 'Right! Give the sailors their orders. Quick or we'll be shipwrecked. Hurry up!'*

Exit. Enter MARINERS.

BOATSWAIN Heigh, my hearts! Cheerly, cheerly, my hearts! Yare, yare! Take in the topsail. Tend to th' master's whistle! Blow till thou burst thy wind, if room enough.   5

> *5-7 'Don't worry lads! Hurry! Take in the topsail and listen to the master's whistle!' The master blew a whistle to give orders — it was easier than shouting in a storm.*

> *7-8 The boatswain's daring the wind to blow even harder.*

Enter ALONSO, SEBASTIAN, ANTONIO, FERDINAND, GONZALO and others

ALONSO Good boatswain, have care. Where's the master? Play the men!   10

> *10 'Get the men to work!'*

BOATSWAIN I pray now, keep below.

> *11 'Please go back down to your cabin.'*

ANTONIO Where is the master, boatswain?

BOATSWAIN Do you not hear him? You mar our labour. Keep your cabins — you do assist the storm.

> *13 'Can't you hear his whistle? You're getting in the way.'*

GONZALO Nay, good, be patient.   15

BOATSWAIN When the sea is. Hence! What cares these roarers for the name of king? To cabin! Silence! Trouble us not.

> *Hence = Go away*

> *roarers = howling waves*

GONZALO Good, yet remember whom thou hast aboard.

> *19 'Careful. Remember you've got a king on board.'*

BOATSWAIN None that I more love than myself. You are a councillor. If you can command these elements to silence, and work the peace of the present, we will not hand a rope more. Use your authority. If you cannot, give thanks you have lived so long, and make yourself ready in your cabin for the mischance of the hour, if it so hap. — Cheerly, good hearts! — Out of our way, I say.   20   25

> *20-23 'You're the King's advisor. If you can advise the storm to stop, we'll give up sailing.' Basically he's saying — you do your job and we'll do ours.*

> *mischance = misfortune*

Exit

GONZALO I have great comfort from this fellow. Methinks he hath no drowning mark upon him — his complexion is perfect gallows. Stand fast, good Fate, to his hanging; make the rope of his destiny our cable, for our own doth little advantage. If he be not born to be hanged, our case is miserable.   30

> *27-32 'I think we're going to be all right. This chap looks to me like someone doomed to die by hanging so I'm sure he won't drown. If I'm wrong we're in trouble.'*

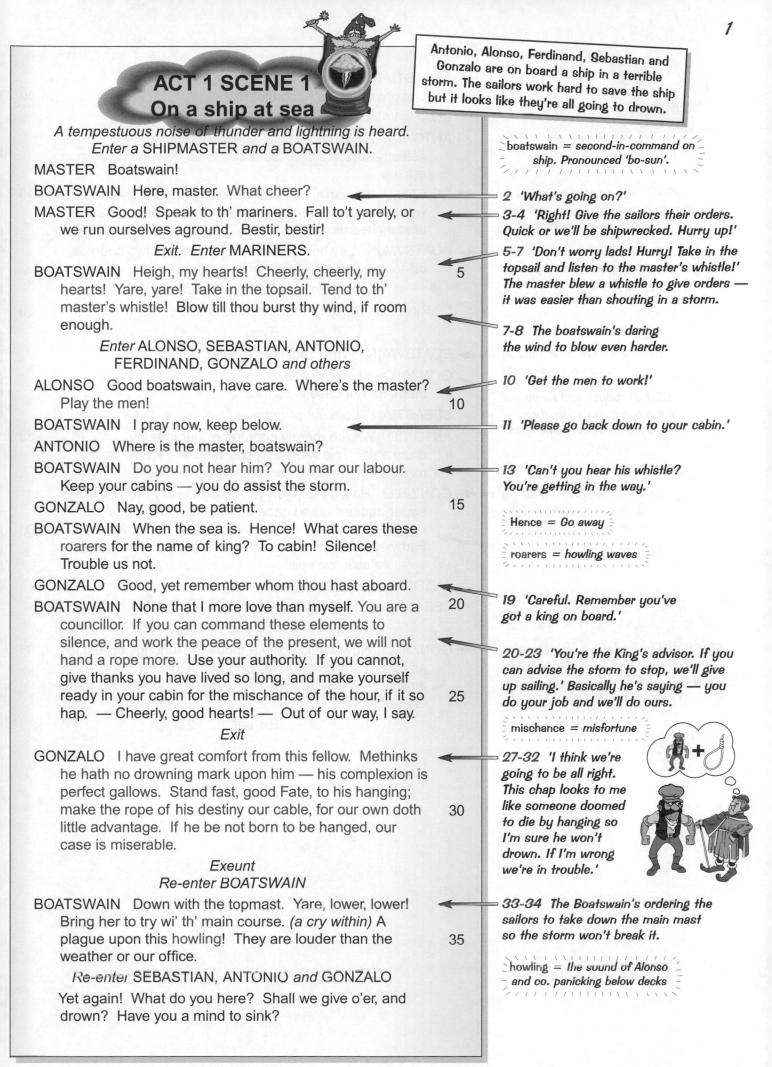

Exeunt
Re-enter BOATSWAIN

BOATSWAIN Down with the topmast. Yare, lower, lower! Bring her to try wi' th' main course. *(a cry within)* A plague upon this howling! They are louder than the weather or our office.   35

> *33-34 The Boatswain's ordering the sailors to take down the main mast so the storm won't break it.*

> *howling = the sound of Alonso and co. panicking below decks*

Re-enter SEBASTIAN, ANTONIO and GONZALO

Yet again! What do you here? Shall we give o'er, and drown? Have you a mind to sink?

cur = dog

45-47 'I guarantee he wouldn't drown, even if the ship was flimsy as a nutshell and really leaky.'

48-49 'Point the ship out to sea again!' He's trying to avoid smashing into the shore.

51 'Are we not even allowed to say our prayers?'

52-53 'Alonso and Ferdinand are praying. Let's join them — we're all in the same boat.'

wide-chopped = big-mouthed

58-59 'I'm sure he'll die by hanging, however hard the water tries to drown him.'

60 'The boat's breaking up!'

take leave of him = say goodbye

65-68 'I'd rather have a little scrap of barren ground than a huge expanse of ocean. There's no escaping fate, but I'd much rather die on dry land.'

fain = rather

SEBASTIAN A pox o' your throat, you bawling, blasphemous, incharitable dog! 40

BOATSWAIN Work you, then.

ANTONIO Hang, cur! Hang, you whoreson, insolent noisemaker! We are less afraid to be drowned than thou art.

GONZALO I'll warrant him for drowning, though the ship were no stronger than a nutshell, and as leaky as an unstanched wench. 45

BOATSWAIN Lay her a-hold, a-hold! Set her two courses off to sea again! Lay her off!

Enter MARINERS, *wet*

MARINERS All lost! To prayers, to prayers! All lost! 50

Exeunt

BOATSWAIN What, must our mouths be cold?

GONZALO The King and Prince at prayers, let's assist them, for our case is as theirs.

SEBASTIAN I am out of patience.

ANTONIO We are merely cheated of our lives by drunkards. This wide-chopped rascal — would thou mightst lie drowning the washing of ten tides! 55

GONZALO He'll be hanged yet, though every drop of water swear against it, and gape at wid'st to glut him. *(a confused noise within)* Mercy on us! We split, we split! Farewell, my wife and children! Farewell, brother! We split, we split, we split! 60

ANTONIO Let's all sink wi' th' King.

SEBASTIAN Let's take leave of him.

Exeunt ANTONIO *and* SEBASTIAN

GONZALO Now would I give a thousand furlongs of sea for an acre of barren ground, long heath, brown furze, anything. The wills above be done, but I would fain die a dry death. 65

Exeunt

Miranda's worried about the shipwreck. Prospero explains it was all part of a plan he's got. He tells Miranda he used to be Duke of Milan. The people who kicked him out are on the ship and he wants a word with them.

ACT 1 SCENE 2
Before Prospero's cell
Enter PROSPERO and MIRANDA

MIRANDA If by your art, my dearest father, you have
  Put the wild waters in this roar, allay them.
  The sky, it seems, would pour down stinking pitch,
  But that the sea, mounting to th' welkin's cheek,
  Dashes the fire out. O, I have suffered   5
  With those that I saw suffer! A brave vessel,
  Who had no doubt some noble creature in her,
  Dashed all to pieces! O, the cry did knock
  Against my very heart! Poor souls, they perished.
  Had I been any god of power, I would   10
  Have sunk the sea within the earth or ere
  It should the good ship so have swallowed and
  The fraughting souls within her.

PROSPERO   Be collected.
  No more amazement. Tell your piteous heart
  There's no harm done.

MIRANDA   O, woe the day!

PROSPERO   No harm.   15
  I have done nothing but in care of thee,
  Of thee, my dear one, thee, my daughter, who
  Art ignorant of what thou art, nought knowing
  Of whence I am, nor that I am more better
  Than Prospero, master of a full poor cell,   20
  And thy no greater father.

MIRANDA   More to know
  Did never meddle with my thoughts.

PROSPERO   'Tis time
  I should inform thee farther. Lend thy hand,
  And pluck my magic garment from me. So,
     (lays down his mantle)
  Lie there my art. Wipe thou thine eyes. Have comfort. 25
  The direful spectacle of the wreck, which touched
  The very virtue of compassion in thee,
  I have with such provision in mine art
  So safely ordered that there is no soul —
  No, not so much perdition as an hair,   30
  Betid to any creature in the vessel
  Which thou heard'st cry, which thou saw'st sink. Sit down,
  For thou must now know farther.

MIRANDA   You have often
  Begun to tell me what I am, but stopped,
  And left me to a bootless inquisition,   35
  Concluding 'Stay, not yet.'

PROSPERO   The hour's now come,
  The very minute bids thee ope thine ear.
  Obey, and be attentive. Canst thou remember
  A time before we came unto this cell?
  I do not think thou canst, for then thou wast not 40
  Out three years old.

cell = cave

1-13 'Dad, if it was you who started this awful storm I wish you'd stop it. The poor people on that ship must have drowned. I felt so sorry for them. If I was some powerful god I would have made the earth swallow the sea, rather than let the sea swallow the ship.'

13-15 'Calm down. Everything's fine.'

15-17 'There's no harm done. It's all for your benefit, dearie'

17-21 'you don't know who you are, where I come from, or that I'm more important than Prospero, your dad who lives in a crummy cave.'

thy = your

21-22 'I never wanted to know more.'

22-24 'It's time you found out the truth. Help me take off my magic cloak.'

26-33 'The shipwreck looked terrible, and it really upset you, but I've arranged the whole thing so carefully that nobody on board that ship has lost as much as a hair from his head. Sit down and I'll tell you more.'

perdition = disaster

33-36 'You've often started to tell me my life story, and then stopped, leaving all my questions unanswered.'

bootless inquisition = pointless question

38-41 'Can you remember a time before we lived in this cave? I don't think you can, because you weren't even three years old.'

MIRANDA   Certainly, sir, I can.

PROSPERO   By what? By any other house, or person?

Of any thing the image, tell me, that
Hath kept with thy remembrance?

MIRANDA   'Tis far off,
And rather like a dream than an assurance   45
That my remembrance warrants. Had I not
Four, or five, women once, that tended me?

PROSPERO   Thou hadst, and more, Miranda. But how is it
That this lives in thy mind? What see'st thou else
In the dark backward and abysm of time?   50
If thou rememb'rest aught, ere thou cam'st here,
How thou cam'st here thou mayst.

MIRANDA   But that I do not.

PROSPERO   Twelve year since, Miranda, twelve year since,
Thy father was the Duke of Milan, and   55

A prince of power.

MIRANDA   Sir, are not you my father?

PROSPERO   Thy mother was a piece of virtue, and
She said thou wast my daughter, and thy father
Was Duke of Milan, and his only heir
And princess, no worse issued.

MIRANDA   O, the heavens!   60

What foul play had we that we came from thence?
Or blessed was't we did?

PROSPERO   Both, both, my girl.

By foul play, as thou say'st, were we heaved thence,
But blessedly holp hither.

MIRANDA   O, my heart bleeds
To think o' th' teen that I have turned you to,   65
Which is from my remembrance. Please you, farther.

PROSPERO   My brother and thy uncle, called Antonio
— I pray thee, mark me that a brother should
Be so perfidious, he, whom next thyself
Of all the world I loved — and to him put   70
The manage of my state, as at that time

Through all the signories it was the first,
And Prospero the prime duke, being so reputed
In dignity, and for the liberal arts
Without a parallel, those being all my study —   75
The government I cast upon my brother
And to my state grew stranger, being transported
And rapt in secret studies. Thy false uncle —
Dost thou attend me?

MIRANDA   Sir, most heedfully.

PROSPERO   Being once perfected how to grant suits,   80
How to deny them, who t' advance, and who
To trash for over-topping, new created
The creatures that were mine, I say, or changed 'em,
Or else new formed 'em, having both the key

Of officer and office, set all hearts i' th' state 85
To what tune pleased his ear, that now he was
The ivy which had hid my princely trunk
And sucked my verdure out on't — Thou attend'st not.

MIRANDA O, good sir, I do!

PROSPERO   I pray thee, mark me.
I thus neglecting worldly ends, all dedicated 90
To closeness and the bettering of my mind
With that which, but by being so retired,
O'er-prized all popular rate, in my false brother
Awaked an evil nature, and my trust,
Like a good parent, did beget of him 95
A falsehood, in its contrary as great
As my trust was, which had indeed no limit,
A confidence sans bound. He being thus lorded,
Not only with what my revenue yielded,
But what my power might else exact, like one 100
Who having into truth, by telling of it,
Made such a sinner of his memory,
To credit his own lie, he did believe
He was indeed the Duke, out o' th' substitution,
And executing th' outward face of royalty 105
With all prerogative. Hence his ambition growing —
Dost thou hear?

MIRANDA   Your tale, sir, would cure deafness.

PROSPERO To have no screen between this part he played
And him he played it for, he needs will be
Absolute Milan. Me, poor man, my library 110
Was dukedom large enough. Of temporal royalties
He thinks me now incapable, confederates —
So dry he was for sway — wi' th' King of Naples,
To give him annual tribute, do him homage,
Subject his coronet to his crown, and bend 115
The dukedom, yet unbowed — alas, poor Milan! —
To most ignoble stooping.

MIRANDA   O the heavens!

PROSPERO Mark his condition, and th' event, then tell me
If this might be a brother.

MIRANDA   I should sin
To think but nobly of my grandmother: 120
Good wombs have borne bad sons.

PROSPERO   Now the condition:
This King of Naples, being an enemy
To me inveterate, hearkens my brother's suit,
Which was, that he, in lieu o' th' premises,
Of homage, and I know not how much tribute, 125
Should presently extirpate me and mine
Out of the dukedom, and confer fair Milan
With all the honours on my brother. Whereon,
A treacherous army levied, one midnight
Fated to th' purpose, did Antonio open 130

verdure = health, freshness

90-98 'I cut myself off completely from the real world and got all wrapped up in my private studies. Left to his own devices my brother developed an evil streak. I trusted him too much and he repaid my trust with lies.'

98-106 'He was having such a great time, living on my money and using my power, that he started to believe he really was the Duke of Milan.'

108-117 'Antonio wanted to be Duke for real. I was busy in my library and he thought I was no good for real-life politics anymore. He made an alliance with Alonso, the King of Naples, offering to pay him money every year if Alonso would support him in taking over Milan.'

ignoble = shameful

118-119 'Is that any way for a brother to behave?'

119-121 'It would be an insult to my grandmother if I said he must have had a different father. Good women have had bad sons.'

121-133 'This is the agreement they made. The King of Naples was an old enemy of mine and he liked Antonio's suggestion. They agreed to get rid of me, so Antonio could be Duke of Milan. They raised an army, and one night at midnight, Antonio opened the city gates and let them in. They captured you and me and hurried us away.'

extirpate = banish

Act 1, Scene 2

6

The gates of Milan, and, i' th' dead of darkness,
The ministers for th' purpose hurried thence
Me and thy crying self.

MIRANDA   Alack, for pity!
I, not rememb'ring how I cried out then,
Will cry it o'er again; it is a hint   135
That wrings mine eyes to't.

PROSPERO   Hear a little further,
And then I'll bring thee to the present business
Which now's upon 's, without the which this story
Were most impertinent.

MIRANDA   Wherefore did they not
That hour destroy us?

PROSPERO   Well demanded, wench!   140
My tale provokes that question. Dear, they durst not,
So dear the love my people bore me, nor set
A mark so bloody on the business, but
With colours fairer painted their foul ends.
In few, they hurried us aboard a bark,   145
Bore us some leagues to sea, where they prepared
A rotten carcass of a butt, not rigged,
Nor tackle, sail, nor mast. The very rats
Instinctively have quit it. There they hoist us,
To cry to th' sea, that roared to us, to sigh   150
To th' winds, whose pity, sighing back again,
Did us but loving wrong.

MIRANDA   Alack, what trouble
Was I then to you!

PROSPERO   O, a cherubin
Thou wast that did preserve me! Thou didst smile,
Infused with a fortitude from heaven,   155
When I have decked the sea with drops full salt,
Under my burden groaned, which raised in me
An undergoing stomach, to bear up
Against what should ensue.

MIRANDA How came we ashore?

PROSPERO   By Providence divine.   160
Some food we had and some fresh water that
A noble Neapolitan, Gonzalo,
Out of his charity, who being then appointed
Master of this design, did give us, with
Rich garments, linens, stuffs, and necessaries,   165
Which since have steaded much. So, of his gentleness,
Knowing I loved my books, he furnished me
From mine own library with volumes that
I prize above my dukedom.

MIRANDA   Would I might
But ever see that man!

PROSPERO   Now I arise. *(puts on his mantle)*   170
Sit still, and hear the last of our sea-sorrow.

134-136 'I can't remember crying then, but it's making me want to cry now.'

136-138 'Just listen a little bit longer and I'll tell you how this all fits in with what's going on right now.'

impertinent = irrelevant

139-140 'Why didn't they just kill us?'

140-144 'Good question! They didn't dare. I was too popular with my subjects. The plotters didn't want to make themselves look too bad.'

145-152 'They put us on board a ship and sailed it out to sea, then set us adrift in a rotten old tub with no sail or anything. Even the rats had deserted it. They abandoned us there in the wind and the waves.'

153-159 'You were an angel and you helped me keep myself together. You smiled when I was crying, and it kept me going through all our trouble.'

fortitude = strength

160-169 'It was luck. We had food, water, clothes and other useful things, given to us by a man from Naples called Gonzalo who was given the job of getting rid of us. He was even kind enough to give me some books from my library.'

169-170 'I'd like to meet him!'

Act 1, Scene 2

Here in this island we arrived, and here
Have I, thy schoolmaster, made thee more profit
Than other princes can, that have more time
For vainer hours, and tutors not so careful. 175

MIRANDA Heavens thank you for't! And now, I pray you, sir,
For still 'tis beating in my mind, your reason
For raising this sea-storm?

PROSPERO   Know thus far forth:
By accident most strange, bountiful Fortune,
Now my dear lady, hath mine enemies 180
Brought to this shore, and by my prescience
I find my zenith doth depend upon
A most auspicious star, whose influence
If now I court not, but omit, my fortunes
Will ever after droop. Here cease more questions. 185
Thou art inclined to sleep. 'Tis a good dullness,
And give it way. I know thou canst not choose.

                    MIRANDA sleeps

 Come away, servant, come! I am ready now.
Approach, my Ariel. Come.

                    Enter ARIEL

ARIEL All hail, great master! Grave sir, hail! I come 190
To answer thy best pleasure — be't to fly,
To swim, to dive into the fire, to ride
On the curled clouds. To thy strong bidding task
Ariel and all his quality.

PROSPERO   Hast thou, spirit,
Performed to point the tempest that I bade thee? 195

ARIEL To every article.
I boarded the King's ship. Now on the beak,
Now in the waist, the deck, in every cabin,
I flamed amazement. Sometime I'd divide
And burn in many places — on the topmast, 200
The yards, and bowsprit, would I flame distinctly,
Then meet and join. Jove's lightning, the precursors
O' th' dreadful thunder-claps, more momentary
And sight-outrunning were not; the fire and cracks
Of sulphurous roaring the most mighty Neptune 205
Seem to besiege, and make his bold waves tremble,
Yea, his dread trident shake.

PROSPERO   My brave spirit!
Who was so firm, so constant, that this coil
Would not infect his reason?

ARIEL   Not a soul
But felt a fever of the mad, and played 210
Some tricks of desperation. All but mariners
Plunged in the foaming brine, and quit the vessel,
Then all afire with me. The King's son, Ferdinand,
With hair up-staring (then like reeds, not hair)
Was the first man that leapt, cried 'Hell is empty, 215
And all the devils are here.'

172-175 'Here I've been your schoolmaster and given you a better education than most princes get.'

bountiful Fortune = good luck

179-187 'By some strange accident, Fortune has brought my enemies to this island. My magical powers tell me that the stars are looking good for me, and if I don't take action now the rest of my life will get worse and worse. That's enough questions for now. Have a little nap.'

auspicious = lucky

Prospero calls his spirit-helper Ariel. Ariel doesn't want to work for Prospero any more, but Prospero promises to let him go if he helps for another two days.

hail = greetings

be't = be it

193-194 'Give me and all the other spirits your orders.'

194-195 'Did you organise the storm exactly as I told you to?'

to every article = right down to the last detail

waist = middle   beak = front end

199-207 'I made myself look like flames, amazing the crew. Sometimes I split myself up, burning in many places around the ship, then joined myself back together. I was faster than Jove's lightning; and the thunder seemed to make Neptune's waves and trident shake.' Jove was Roman god of the sky, Neptune was god of the sea.

208-209 'Was anyone brave enough to stand all the racket without going a bit mad?'

brine = sea

quit the vessel = jumped over board

Act 1, Scene 2

nigh = near

218-225 *'Nobody lost a hair. Their clothes are even cleaner than they were before. I've done what you said and scattered them in little groups around the island. Ferdinand's sitting all alone in a quiet corner, sighing and twisting his arms in knots.'*

225-227 *'What have you done with the ship and the sailors and the rest of the fleet?'*

still-vexed = still troubled by reefs and storms that were dangerous for ships

231-233 *'The sailors are below decks. I cast a spell and they're worn out anyway so they're all fast asleep.'*

233-238 *'The rest of the fleet was scattered but now they've met up again and they're sailing back across the Mediterranean to Naples, all sad because they think the King and his ship are lost.'*

mid-season = noon

241-242 *'It's at least two. You and I have got to make the most of the time between now and six.'*

243-245 *'Is there more work to do? Let me remind you that you've made me a promise and you haven't kept it.'*

How now = hello

liberty = freedom

I prithee = I pray you, I beg you

or = either

bate me = let me off

PROSPERO   Why, that's my spirit!
But was not this nigh shore?

ARIEL   Close by, my master.

PROSPERO   But are they, Ariel, safe?

ARIEL   Not a hair perished,
On their sustaining garments not a blemish,
But fresher than before, and, as thou bad'st me,   220
In troops I have dispersed them 'bout the isle.
The King's son have I landed by himself,
Whom I left cooling of the air with sighs
In an odd angle of the isle, and sitting,
His arms in this sad knot.

PROSPERO   Of the King's ship,   225
The mariners, say how thou hast disposed,
And all the rest o' th' fleet?

ARIEL   Safely in harbour
Is the King's ship. In the deep nook, where once
Thou called'st me up at midnight to fetch dew
From the still-vexed Bermudas, there she's hid;   230
The mariners all under hatches stowed,
Who, with a charm joined to their suffered labour,
I have left asleep; and for the rest o' th' fleet,
Which I dispersed, they all have met again,
And are upon the Mediterranean float   235
Bound sadly home for Naples,
Supposing that they saw the King's ship wrecked,
And his great person perish.

PROSPERO   Ariel, thy charge
Exactly is performed, but there's more work.
What is the time o' th' day?

ARIEL   Past the mid-season.   240

PROSPERO   At least two glasses. The time 'twixt six and now
Must by us both be spent most preciously.

ARIEL   Is there more toil? Since thou dost give me pains,
Let me remember thee what thou hast promised,
Which is not yet performed me.

PROSPERO   How now, moody?   245
What is't thou canst demand?

ARIEL   My liberty.

PROSPERO   Before the time be out? No more!

ARIEL   I prithee,
Remember I have done thee worthy service,
Told thee no lies, made thee no mistakings, served
Without or grudge or grumblings. Thou didst promise   250
To bate me a full year.

PROSPERO   Dost thou forget
From what a torment I did free thee?

ARIEL   No.

PROSPERO   Thou dost, and think'st it much to tread the ooze
    Of the salt deep,
    To run upon the sharp wind of the north,   255
    To do me business in the veins o' th' earth
    When it is baked with frost.

ARIEL   I do not, sir.

PROSPERO   Thou liest, malignant thing. Hast thou forgot
    The foul witch Sycorax, who with age and envy
    Was grown into a hoop? Hast thou forgot her?

ARIEL   No, sir.   260

PROSPERO   Thou hast. Where was she born? Speak! Tell me.

ARIEL   Sir, in Algiers.

PROSPERO   O, was she so? I must
    Once in a month recount what thou hast been,
    Which thou forget'st. This damned witch Sycorax,
    For mischiefs manifold, and sorceries terrible   265
    To enter human hearing, from Algiers
    Thou know'st was banished. For one thing she did
    They would not take her life. Is not this true?

ARIEL   Ay, sir.

PROSPERO   This blue-eyed hag was hither brought with child,
    And here was left by th'sailors. Thou, my slave,   270
    As thou report'st thyself, wast then her servant;
    And, for thou wast a spirit too delicate
    To act her earthy and abhorred commands,
    Refusing her grand hests, she did confine thee,
    By help of her more potent ministers,   275
    And in her most unmitigable rage,
    Into a cloven pine, within which rift
    Imprisoned, thou didst painfully remain
    A dozen years, within which space she died,
    And left thee there, where thou didst vent thy groans   280
    As fast as mill-wheels strike. Then was this island —
    Save for the son that she did litter here,
    A freckled whelp, hag-born — not honoured with
    A human shape.

ARIEL   Yes, Caliban her son.

PROSPERO   Dull thing, I say so — he, that Caliban   285
    Whom now I keep in service. Thou best know'st
    What torment I did find thee in. Thy groans
    Did make wolves howl, and penetrate the breasts
    Of ever-angry bears. It was a torment
    To lay upon the damned, which Sycorax   290
    Could not again undo. It was mine art,
    When I arrived and heard thee, that made gape
    The pine, and let thee out.

ARIEL   I thank thee, master.

PROSPERO   If thou more murmur'st, I will rend an oak
    And peg thee in his knotty entrails, till   295
    Thou hast howled away twelve winters.

253-257 'You've forgotten what I freed you from. You think it's a burden to fly across the ocean, run with the wind and go into the warm depths of the earth when the surface is covered in frost.'

malignant = poisonous

258-260 'Have you forgotten the horrid witch Sycorax, who was so twisted that her body was shaped like a hoop?'

264-268 'As you know, Sycorax was exiled from Algiers for all the wicked, unspeakable things she'd done. They wouldn't kill her because she'd once helped the town.'

with child = pregnant

272-284 'You were too delicate to carry out her rough and nasty orders. She got into a terrible rage, and with the help of some other spirits, trapped you in a pine tree. You stayed there for a dozen years and in that time she died and left you there, groaning away. There wasn't one other person here then, except her deformed child.'

unmitigable = uncontrollable

ow!

Dull thing = stupid creature

in service = as my servant

289-293 'It was the kind of punishment damned souls get in hell and even Sycorax couldn't undo her spell. It was my skills that got you out of the pine tree.'

294-295 'If you complain again I'll rip open an oak tree and trap you inside its woody guts'

Act 1, Scene 2

ARIEL   Pardon, master.
    I will be correspondent to command,
    And do my spriting gently.

correspondent = obedient

Ariel's new disguise

PROSPERO   Do so, and after two days
    I will discharge thee.

ARIEL   That's my noble master!   300
    What shall I do? Say what. What shall I do?

302-305 'Go and disguise yourself like a sea fairy. Make yourself invisible to everyone except you and me. Go and disguise yourself then come back.'

PROSPERO   Go make thyself like a nymph o' th' sea.
    Be subject to no sight but thine and mine, invisible
    To every eyeball else. Go take this shape,
    And hither come in 't. Go, hence with diligence!   305

diligence = care

Exit ARIEL

    Awake, dear heart, awake, thou hast slept well.
    Awake.

MIRANDA   The strangeness of your story put
    Heaviness in me.

Heaviness = sleepiness

PROSPERO   Shake it off. Come on,
    We'll visit Caliban, my slave, who never   310
    Yields us kind answer.

Yields = gives

MIRANDA   'Tis a villain, sir,
    I do not love to look on.

villain = low-born man, peasant

312-315 'We can't do without him. He makes the fire, fetches the wood in. He's very useful.'

PROSPERO   But as 'tis,
    We cannot miss him: he does make our fire,
    Fetch in our wood, and serves in offices
    That profit us. What ho! Slave! Caliban!   315
    Thou earth, thou! Speak.

earth = stupid lump

within = inside, in the cave

CALIBAN *(within)*   There's wood enough within.

like a water-nymph = Ariel has changed shape

PROSPERO   Come forth, I say. There's other business for thee.
    Come, thou tortoise! When?

            Re-enter ARIEL *like a water-nymph*

    Fine apparition! My quaint Ariel,
    Hark in thine ear.   *(Whispers)*

320 'Listen to this.'

ARIEL   My lord, it shall be done.   320

            Exit

PROSPERO   Thou poisonous slave, got by the devil himself
    Upon thy wicked dam, come forth!

got = fathered

dam = mother

come forth = come out

            Enter CALIBAN

323-326 Caliban's cursing Prospero and Miranda, hoping they'll be covered with poisonous dew and get nasty blisters.

CALIBAN   As wicked dew as e'er my mother brushed
    With raven's feather from unwholesome fen
    Drop on you both! A south-west blow on ye   325
    And blister you all o'er!

327-332 'For that you'll have cramps tonight, and stitches that don't let you breathe. All night long goblins will work you over, pinching you till your skin is swollen and painful.'

PROSPERO   For this, be sure, tonight thou shalt have cramps,
    Side-stitches that shall pen thy breath up, urchins
    Shall, for that vast of night that they may work,
    All exercise on thee, thou shalt be pinched   330
    As thick as honeycomb, each pinch more stinging
    Than bees that made 'em.

CALIBAN   I must eat my dinner.
   This island's mine, by Sycorax my mother,
   Which thou tak'st from me. When thou cam'st first,
   Thou strok'st me and made much of me, wouldst give me   335
   Water with berries in't, and teach me how
   To name the bigger light, and how the less,
   That burn by day and night, and then I loved thee,
   And showed thee all the qualities o' th' isle,
   The fresh springs, brine-pits, barren place and fertile.   340
   Cursed be I that did so! All the charms
   Of Sycorax, toads, beetles, bats, light on you!
   For I am all the subjects that you have,
   Which first was mine own king, and here you sty me
   In this hard rock, whiles you do keep from me   345
   The rest o' th' island.

PROSPERO   Thou most lying slave,
   Whom stripes may move, not kindness! I have used thee,
   Filth as thou art, with human care, and lodged thee
   In mine own cell, till thou didst seek to violate
   The honour of my child.   350

CALIBAN O ho, o ho! Would't had been done.
   Thou didst prevent me — I had peopled else
   This isle with Calibans.

MIRANDA   Abhorred slave,
   Which any print of goodness wilt not take,
   Being capable of all ill! I pitied thee,   355
   Took pains to make thee speak, taught thee each hour
   One thing or other. When thou didst not, savage,
   Know thine own meaning, but wouldst gabble like
   A thing most brutish, I endowed thy purposes
   With words that made them known. But thy vile race,   360
   Though thou didst learn, had that in't which good natures
   Could not abide to be with. Therefore wast thou
   Deservedly confined into this rock, who hadst
   Deserved more than a prison.

CALIBAN You taught me language, and my profit on't   365
   Is, I know how to curse. The red plague rid you
   For learning me your language!

PROSPERO   Hag-seed, hence!
   Fetch us in fuel. And be quick, thou 'rt best,
   To answer other business. Shrugg'st thou, malice?
   If thou neglect'st, or dost unwillingly   370
   What I command, I'll rack thee with old cramps,
   Fill all thy bones with aches, make thee roar,
   That beasts shall tremble at thy din.

CALIBAN   No, pray thee.
   (aside) I must obey. His art is of such power,
   It would control my dam's god, Setebos,   375
   And make a vassal of him.

PROSPERO   So, slave, hence!
                  Exit CALIBAN.

Margin notes:

333-340 'This is my island, inherited from my mother Sycorax, and you've taken it from me. When you first came you were kind to me, and made me drinks and taught me about the sun and moon. I loved you for it. I showed you where to find water and fertile land.'

343-345 'I used to be king here. Now I'm your only subject and you keep me trapped in this nasty cave'

stripes = blows with a whip

347-350 'Disgusting as you are, I treated you with human kindness and let you live in my own cave until you tried to rape Miranda.'

351-353 'I wish I had. If you hadn't stopped me I would have filled the whole island with Calibans.'

353-360 'You horrible slave! Goodness can have no influence on you. I felt sorry for you, taught you things, taught you how to speak.'

360-364 'You learnt some things but no good person could bear to be with someone like you. You deserve to live in this rock. You deserved worse than prison.'

365-367 'You taught me how to speak and now I know how to curse. A plague on you for teaching me your language!'

367 'Get lost, witchboy!'

din = noise

374-376 'His magic is so powerful that it would make a slave out of my mother's spirit-master, Setebos.'

Ariel leads Ferdinand in. It's love at first sight for Miranda and Ferdinand. Prospero's pleased but he wants to test them so he pretends to think Ferdinand's a spy and gets really angry.

Re-enter ARIEL invisible, playing and singing, FERDINAND following.

377-383 The words are like instructions for dancers. *'Come onto the yellow sands and take your partners' hands. Curtsy, kiss and when the wild waves are hushed, dance neatly here and there. The sweet spirits sing the chorus. Listen, listen!'*

ARIEL *(sings)* Come unto these yellow sands,
And then take hands;
Curtsied when you have and kissed,
The wild waves whist,   380
Foot it featly here and there,
And, sweet sprites, the burden bear.
Hark, hark!

SPIRITS *(dispersedly)* Bow-wow.

ARIEL The watch dogs bark.   385

SPIRITS *(dispersedly)* Bow-wow.

387-388 *'I hear the cry of a strutting cockerel'*

ARIEL Hark, hark! I hear
The strain of strutting chanticleer
Cry, Cock-a-diddle-dow.

390-396 *'Where's this music coming from, the air or the earth? It's gone, probably to play for some god of the island. I was sitting on a river bank weeping for my father when the music floated by. It calmed the waves and my emotions and I've followed it here.'*

FERDINAND Where should this music be? I' th' air or th' earth?
It sounds no more, and sure it waits upon
Some god o' th' island. Sitting on a bank,
Weeping again the King my father's wreck,
This music crept by me upon the waters,
Allaying both their fury and my passion   395
With its sweet air. Thence I have followed it,
Or it hath drawn me rather. But 'tis gone.
No, it begins again.

399-405 *'Your father's body is lying thirty feet under water. His bones have turned to coral, his eyes have turned to pearls. He is not fading away; the sea is changing him into something rich and strange. Every hour sea nymphs ring bells for him.'*

ARIEL *(sings)* Full fathom five thy father lies;
Of his bones are coral made;   400
Those are pearls that were his eyes;
Nothing of him that doth fade
But doth suffer a sea-change
Into something rich and strange.
Sea-nymphs hourly ring his knell: 405

SPIRITS Ding-dong.

ARIEL Hark! Now I hear them. Ding dong bell.

408-410 *'It's a song about my dad. This is the work of some sort of spirit, not a sound made here on earth.'*

FERDINAND The ditty does remember my drowned father.
This is no mortal business, nor no sound
That the earth owes. I hear it now above me.   410

411-412 *'What do you see through those lovely lashes, Miranda?'*

PROSPERO The fringed curtains of thine eye advance,
And say what thou seest yond.

MIRANDA   What is't? A spirit?

413-414 *'I think it's very handsome dad. But it's definitely a spirit.'*

Lord, how it looks about! Believe me, sir,
It carries a brave form. But 'tis a spirit.

PROSPERO No, wench — it eats and sleeps and hath such   415
senses

416-420 *'This handsome fellow was in the shipwreck. He's a bit upset at the moment so he isn't looking his best, but he's a decent person. He's looking for his friends.'*

As we have, such. This gallant which thou seest
Was in the wreck, and but he's something stained
With grief, that's beauty's canker, thou mightst call him
A goodly person. He hath lost his fellows,
And strays about to find 'em.

MIRANDA   I might call him   420
A thing divine, for nothing natural
I ever saw so noble.

PROSPERO *(aside)*   It goes on, I see,
As my soul prompts it. Spirit, fine spirit! I'll free thee
Within two days for this.

FERDINAND   Most sure, the goddess
On whom these airs attend! Vouchsafe my pray'r   425
May know if you remain upon this island,
And that you will some good instruction give
How I may bear me here. My prime request,
Which I do last pronounce, is — O you wonder! —
If you be maid or no?

MIRANDA   No wonder, sir —   430
But certainly a maid.

FERDINAND   My language? Heavens!
I am the best of them that speak this speech,
Were I but where 'tis spoken.

PROSPERO   How the best?
What wert thou, if the King of Naples heard thee?

FERDINAND   A single thing, as I am now, that wonders   435
To hear thee speak of Naples. He does hear me,
And that he does I weep. Myself am Naples,
Who with mine eyes, never since at ebb, beheld
The King my father wrecked.

MIRANDA   Alack, for mercy!

FERDINAND   Yes, faith, and all his lords, the Duke of Milan   440
And his brave son being twain.

PROSPERO *(aside)*   The Duke of Milan
And his more braver daughter could control thee,
If now 'twere fit to do't. At the first sight
They have changed eyes. Delicate Ariel,
I'll set thee free for this. *(to FERDINAND)* A word, good sir —
I fear you have done yourself some wrong — a word.

MIRANDA   Why speaks my father so ungently? This
Is the third man that e'er I saw, the first
That e'er I sighed for. Pity move my father
To be inclined my way!

FERDINAND   O, if a virgin,   450
And your affection not gone forth, I'll make you
The Queen of Naples.

PROSPERO   Soft, sir, one word more!
(aside) They are both in either's pow'rs, but this swift business
I must uneasy make, lest too light winning
Make the prize light. *(to FERDINAND)* One word more — I   455
                                   charge thee
That thou attend me — thou dost here usurp
The name thou ow'st not and hast put thyself
Upon this island as a spy, to win it
From me, the lord on't.

FERDINAND   No, as I am a man.

MIRANDA   There's nothing ill can dwell in such a temple.   460
If the ill spirit have so fair a house,
Good things will strive to dwell with't.

422-423
'Excellent, just what I was hoping for.

424-430 'You must be the goddess who all this music is for! Please will you stay here and show me how to survive on this island? And more importantly, are you single?'

431-433 'What a coincidence — you speak the same language as me. If I was in my home country I'd be one of the best speakers of this language.'

433-434 'What do you mean, the best? Would you still be best if the King of Naples was here?'

435-439 'I'd be the same person I am now. I am the King of Naples, and I've been crying about it ever since I saw my father the King die in a shipwreck.'

440-441 'Yup, and all his lords died with him, including Antonio and his son.'

441-444 'The real Duke and his daughter could have complete power over you if now was the moment. I think it's love at first sight.'

448 The first was Prospero and the second was Caliban.

sighed for = *fell in love with*

451 'you're not in love with anyone else.'

453-455 'They're madly in love, but I'd better slow things down a bit. They need a bit of a test.'

456-459 'You're lying. You're not the King of Naples. You're a spy, sent to take this island off me.'

460-462 'He can't be a bad person. He's much too handsome. Even if he's a bit bad I'm sure he's got good bits too.'

14

manacle = chain

468-469 'I won't be treated like that unless it's by force.'

charmed from moving = Prospero puts a spell on Ferdinand to stop him fighting him

470-471 'Don't be too hard on him. He's a nice guy.'

471-476 'Are you trying to lecture your own father? You, traitor, put your sword away. You don't really dare to attack because you've got a guilty conscience. Give up. I can easily disarm you with my wand.'

Beseech you = I beg you

478 'I'll make sure he behaves.'

478-484 'Not another word or I'll be super-furious. Why are you standing up for a fake? You think he's amazing because you've only ever seen him and Caliban. Silly girl — compared to most men he's as ugly as Caliban and they look like angels.'

484-486 'I'll settle for him then. I don't want anything better.'

486-488 'You're in my power now. You're like a weak little baby.'

489-495 'I can't do a thing, just like in a dream. Lots of bad things have happened, but I don't care so long as I can see this gorgeous female once a day from my prison cell. I don't want to be free if I have to be away from her.'

498 'I've got more instructions for you.'

PROSPERO   Follow me.
Speak not you for him — he's a traitor. Come!
I'll manacle thy neck and feet together.
Sea-water shalt thou drink, thy food shall be   465
The fresh-brook mussels, withered roots, and husks
Wherein the acorn cradled. Follow.

FERDINAND   No —
I will resist such entertainment till
Mine enemy has more power.

He draws, and is charmed from moving

MIRANDA   O dear father,
Make not too rash a trial of him, for   470
He's gentle, and not fearful.

PROSPERO   What, I say,
My foot my tutor? Put thy sword up, traitor,
Who mak'st a show but dar'st not strike, thy conscience
Is so possessed with guilt. Come from thy ward,
For I can here disarm thee with this stick   475
And make thy weapon drop.

MIRANDA   Beseech you, father!

PROSPERO Hence! Hang not on my garments.

MIRANDA   Sir, have pity.
I'll be his surety.

PROSPERO   Silence! One word more
Shall make me chide thee, if not hate thee. What!
An advocate for an impostor! Hush!   480
Thou think'st there is no more such shapes as he,
Having seen but him and Caliban. Foolish wench!
To th' most of men this is a Caliban,
And they to him are angels.

MIRANDA   My affections
Are then most humble. I have no ambition   485
To see a goodlier man.

PROSPERO   Come on — obey.
Thy nerves are in their infancy again,
And have no vigour in them.

FERDINAND   So they are.
My spirits, as in a dream, are all bound up.
My father's loss, the weakness which I feel,   490
The wreck of all my friends, nor this man's threats
To whom I am subdued, are but light to me,
Might I but through my prison once a day
Behold this maid. All corners else o' th' earth
Let liberty make use of. Space enough   495
Have I in such a prison.

PROSPERO   (aside) It works. (to FERDINAND)
                                              Come on.
Thou hast done well, fine Ariel!
                         (to FERDINAND) Follow me.
(to ARIEL) Hark what thou else shalt do me.

Act 1, Scene 2

MIRANDA   Be of comfort.   *498-501 'Don't worry, my*
    My father's of a better nature, sir,   *dad's not normally like this.'*
    Than he appears by speech. This is unwonted   500
    Which now came from him.   *unwonted = unusual*

PROSPERO *(to* ARIEL*)*   Thou shalt be as free   *501-503 'You'll be as free as the*
    As mountain winds — but then exactly do   *wind if you do just as I say.'*
    All points of my command.

ARIEL   To th' syllable.

PROSPERO *(to* FERDINAND*)* Come, follow. *(to* MIRANDA*)*   *504 'Stop standing up for him.'*
                        Speak not for him.

                    Exeunt

Act 1 — Revision Summary

Shipwreck, love, creepy monsters — this play's almost as good as Pirates of the Caribbean. Shame we couldn't get Johnny Depp (or Keira Knightley) to star. I did phone their agents, but apparently they don't do books, only films. You'll just have to imagine they're playing Ferdinand and Miranda. Or if that doesn't sound like fun, how about some real old-fashioned entertainment — answer all these questions to check you've understood Act 1. It's not actually fun, but in our survey 8 out of 10 cats agreed it's good for you.

SCENE 1

1) Where does this scene take place?

2) What's a boatswain?

3) Who thinks the boatswain's more likely to hang than to drown?

4) Who calls the boatswain a "bawling, blasphemous, incharitable dog"?

SCENE 2

5) Why is Miranda worried?

6) How old was Miranda when she came to live on the island with Prospero?

7) What is Prospero's brother called?

8) What did the King of Naples help Prospero's brother to do?

9) Why didn't they kill Prospero and Miranda?

10) What did they do instead?

11) Who helped Miranda and Prospero? How did he help them?

12) Does Prospero take an unbelievably long time to tell his story, dragging it out almost beyond belief, and revelling in Miranda's fawning attention?

    a) yes   b) basically, yes   c) absolutely   d) I think you're being a bit harsh, but, well, yes

13) Explain in one sentence why Prospero has created the storm.

14) Describe what Ariel was doing during the storm.

15) Who was first to jump into the sea? Who stayed on the ship?

16) What happened to the people who jumped into the sea? Where did they end up after the storm?

17) Who was Sycorax?

18) What did Sycorax do to Ariel?

19) What relation is Caliban to Sycorax?

20) Prospero tells Ariel to go and change his appearance. What does he want him to look like?

21) Write down three curses Caliban makes against Prospero.

22) When Prospero and Miranda first came to the island they were kind to Caliban and tried to teach him. Why did they change the way they treated him?

23) Why does Caliban obey Prospero?

24) How does Ariel lead Ferdinand to Prospero and Miranda?

25) What does Ferdinand think has happened to his father?

26) What does Miranda think Ferdinand is when she first sees him?

27) Why does Prospero pretend to be cross with Ferdinand? What does he accuse him of?

28) How does Prospero stop Ferdinand from trying to fight him?

29) What does Prospero mean when he tells Miranda, "To th'most of men this is a Caliban"?

30) Why does Ferdinand think it's not going to be so bad to be Prospero's prisoner?

ACT 2 SCENE 1
Another part of the island

Enter ALONSO, SEBASTIAN, ANTONIO,
GONZALO, ADRIAN, FRANCISCO *and others*

GONZALO Beseech you, sir, be merry. You have cause,
   So have we all, of joy, for our escape
   Is much beyond our loss. Our hint of woe
   Is common — every day, some sailor's wife,
   The masters of some merchant and the merchant,   5
   Have just our theme of woe. But for the miracle —
   I mean our preservation — few in millions
   Can speak like us. Then wisely, good sir, weigh
   Our sorrow with our comfort.

ALONSO   Prithee, peace.

SEBASTIAN He receives comfort like cold porridge.   10

ANTONIO The visitor will not give him o'er so.

SEBASTIAN Look, he's winding up the watch of his wit —
   by and by it will strike.

GONZALO Sir —

SEBASTIAN One — tell.   15

GONZALO When every grief is entertained that's offered,
   Comes to th' entertainer —

SEBASTIAN A dollar.

GONZALO Dolour comes to him, indeed. You have spoken
   truer than you purposed.   20

SEBASTIAN You have taken it wiselier than I meant you
   should.

GONZALO Therefore, my lord —

ANTONIO Fie, what a spendthrift is he of his tongue!

ALONSO I prithee, spare.   25

GONZALO Well, I have done — but yet —

SEBASTIAN He will be talking.

ANTONIO Which, of he or Adrian, for a good wager, first
   begins to crow?

SEBASTIAN The old cock.   30

ANTONIO The cock'rel.

SEBASTIAN Done. The wager?

ANTONIO A laughter.

SEBASTIAN A match!

ADRIAN Though this island seem to be desert —   35

ANTONIO Ha, ha, ha!

SEBASTIAN So, you're paid.

ADRIAN Uninhabitable, and almost inaccessible —

SEBASTIAN Yet —

ADRIAN Yet —   40

ANTONIO He could not miss't.

---

beseech = I beg

1-9 'We should all be happy — there are more of us alive than dead. This sort of thing happens all the time to sailors' wives and merchants. The chances of escaping are very slim, so look on the bright side.'

9 'Please shut up.'

visitor = charitable, patronising person   *give him o'er so = let him off so easily*

one = his watch has just struck one

16-17 'If you indulge your emotions...'

dollar = large coin

Dolour = pain, misery

24 'Crikey, he goes on a bit.'

spare = save it, keep it to yourself

28-29 'Let's have a bet. Do you think Adrian or Gonzalo will speak next?'

30 He means Gonzalo.

31 The cockerel is Adrian.

41 'He couldn't resist saying "yet".'

18

42-43 'The landscape and the weather seem OK.'

ADRIAN   It must needs be of subtle, tender and delicate temperance.

44 'Weather was a lovely girl.'

ANTONIO   Temperance was a delicate wench.

45-46 'And a sneaky one. He seems to know her well.'

SEBASTIAN   Ay, and a subtle, as he most learnedly delivered.   45

ADRIAN   The air breathes upon us here most sweetly.

SEBASTIAN   As if it had lungs, and rotten ones.

49 People thought the air in fens and marshes was full of diseases, so somewhere 'perfumed by a fen' would be dangerous and nasty.

ANTONIO   Or, as 'twere perfumed by a fen.

GONZALO   Here is everything advantageous to life.   50

ANTONIO   True — save means to live.

51 'Everything except the things you need to keep you alive.'

SEBASTIAN   Of that there's none, or little.

GONZALO   How lush and lusty the grass looks! How green!

tawny = brown

ANTONIO   The ground indeed is tawny.

SEBASTIAN   With an eye of green in't.   55

ANTONIO   He misses not much.

SEBASTIAN   No, he doth but mistake the truth totally.

58-59 'The thing that's really hard to believe is...'

GONZALO   But the rarity of it is, which is indeed almost beyond credit —

SEBASTIAN   As many vouched rarities are.   60

61-64 'Even though we've all had a good soaking in the sea, our clothes are fresh and dry.'

GONZALO   That our garments, being, as they were, drenched in the sea, hold, notwithstanding, their freshness and glosses, being rather new-dyed, than stained with salt water.

but = just

pocket up = hide away

ANTONIO   If but one of his pockets could speak, would it not say he lies?   65

SEBASTIAN   Ay, or very falsely pocket up his report.

69-70 Alonso and everyone else were on their way back from Claribel's wedding when the shipwreck happened.

GONZALO   Methinks our garments are now as fresh as when we put them on first in Afric, at the marriage of the King's fair daughter Claribel to the King of Tunis.   70

71-72 'It was a lovely wedding, and a super journey home.'

SEBASTIAN   'Twas a sweet marriage, and we prosper well in our return.

73-74 'She's the most perfect queen they've ever had.'

ADRIAN   Tunis was never graced before with such a paragon to their queen.

75, 78, 81 In the famous Latin poem the *Aeneid*, Dido was the queen of Carthage (a city down the coast from Tunis). The hero Aeneas marries Dido, but then runs away so Dido kills herself. A happy tale.

GONZALO   Not since widow Dido's time.   75

ANTONIO   Widow! A pox o' that! How came that 'widow' in? Widow Dido!

SEBASTIAN   What if he had said 'widower Aeneas' too? Good Lord, how you take it!

ADRIAN   'Widow Dido' said you? You make me study of that. She was of Carthage, not of Tunis.   80

GONZALO   This Tunis, sir, was Carthage.

ADRIAN   Carthage?

GONZALO   I assure you, Carthage.

85 In one of the Greek myths, Amphion raised a city out of the ground by playing his harp and singing. Antonio's teasing Gonzalo for getting the name of Dido's home town wrong.

ANTONIO   His word is more than the miraculous harp.   85

SEBASTIAN   He hath raised the wall, and houses too.

ANTONIO   What impossible matter will he make easy next?

SEBASTIAN   I think he will carry this island home in his pocket, and give it his son for an apple.

Act 2, Scene 1

ANTONIO   And, sowing the kernels of it in the sea, bring forth   90
    more islands.

GONZALO   Ay.

ANTONIO   Why, in good time.

GONZALO   Sir, we were talking that our garments seem now
    as fresh as when we were at Tunis at the marriage of your   95
    daughter, who is now Queen.

ANTONIO   And the rarest that e'er came there.

SEBASTIAN   Bate, I beseech you, widow Dido.

ANTONIO   O, widow Dido! Ay, widow Dido.

GONZALO   Is not, sir, my doublet as fresh as the first day I   100
    wore it? I mean, in a sort.

ANTONIO   That 'sort' was well fished for.

GONZALO   When I wore it at your daughter's marriage?

ALONSO   You cram these words into mine ears against
    The stomach of my sense. Would I had never   105
    Married my daughter there, for, coming thence,
    My son is lost, and, in my rate, she too,
    Who is so far from Italy removed
    I ne'er again shall see her. O thou mine heir
    Of Naples and of Milan, what strange fish   110
    Hath made his meal on thee?

FRANCISCO   Sir, he may live.
    I saw him beat the surges under him,
    And ride upon their backs; he trod the water,
    Whose enmity he flung aside, and breasted
    The surge most swoll'n that met him; his bold head   115
    'Bove the contentious waves he kept, and oared
    Himself with his good arms in lusty stroke
    To th' shore, that o'er his wave-worn basis bowed,
    As stooping to relieve him. I not doubt
    He came alive to land.

ALONSO   No, no, he's gone.   120

SEBASTIAN   Sir, you may thank yourself for this great loss,
    That would not bless our Europe with your daughter,
    But rather lose her to an African,
    Where she, at least, is banished from your eye,
    Who hath cause to wet the grief on't.

ALONSO   Prithee, peace.   125

SEBASTIAN   You were kneeled to, and importuned otherwise
    By all of us, and the fair soul herself
    Weighed between loathness and obedience at
    Which end o' th' beam should bow. We have lost your son,
    I fear, for ever. Milan and Naples have   130
    More widows in them of this business' making,
    Than we bring men to comfort them.
    The fault's your own.

ALONSO   So is the dear'st o' th' loss.

GONZALO   My lord Sebastian,
    The truth you speak doth lack some gentleness,   135

rarest = finest

98 'Don't mention the widow Dido.'

doublet = waistcoat

in a sort = pretty much

104-111 'You're forcing me to listen to you but you're not making any sense. I wish I'd never married Claribel to the King of Tunis — my son's been killed on the way home, and she lives so far from Italy now that I'll never see her again. Poor old Ferdinand, I wonder what sort of fish is eating you now?'

112-120 'I saw him swimming for shore with all his strength. I'm sure he reached the land alive.'

contentious = difficult

121-125 'You've brought it all on yourself by marrying your daughter to an African, not keeping her in Europe. At least she's not around to see you crying.'

126-129 'We all begged you not to do it. She was torn between wanting to obey you and not wanting to go.'

130-132 'There are more women in Naples and Milan who've lost husbands in this wreck than men who've survived it.'

133 'I'm the most upset.'

135 'You're right but you're being a bit harsh.'

Act 2, Scene 1

chirurgeonly =
like a surgeon

139-140 'We all feel
down when you do.'

141 'If I was responsible
for colonising this island'

docks, mallows
= weeds

145 'There's no wine so
you couldn't get drunk.'

146-155 'I'd run the country in a
completely new way. There'd be no
business, no judges, no writing, no
wealth or poverty, no servants, no
contracts, no inheritance, no private
farmland or vineyards, no metal, corn,
wine or oil. Nobody would have to work,
men or women, but it wouldn't turn them
bad. There'd be no government...'

155 'Even though he wants to be King.'

158-162 'Nature would give us
everything we needed without any
effort. I wouldn't allow treason,
crime, weapons or machines. Nature
would provide everything I needed'

knaves = wasters

166-167 'If this was my country,
life would be even more perfect
than it was in the golden age.' The
golden age was supposed to be a
perfect time in the distant past.

do you mark me = are
you paying attention

171-174 'I know I was talking nonsense,
but I was trying to give these jokers
something to laugh about.'

178 'That's telling us!'

179 'But in a feeble kind of way.'
A 'flat-long' blow with a sword
was a smack with the flat side.

And time to speak it in. You rub the sore,
When you should bring the plaster.

SEBASTIAN   Very well.

ANTONIO   And most chirurgeonly.

GONZALO   It is foul weather in us all, good sir,
When you are cloudy.

SEBASTIAN   Foul weather?

ANTONIO   Very foul. 140

GONZALO   Had I plantation of this isle, my lord —

ANTONIO   He'd sow 't with nettle-seed.

SEBASTIAN   Or docks, or mallows.

GONZALO   And were the king on't, what would I do?

SEBASTIAN   Scape being drunk for want of wine. 145

GONZALO   I' th' commonwealth I would by contraries
Execute all things; for no kind of traffic
Would I admit; no name of magistrate;
Letters should not be known; riches, poverty,
And use of service, none; contract, succession, 150
Bourn, bound of land, tilth, vineyard, none;
No use of metal, corn, or wine, or oil;
No occupation; all men idle, all;
And women too, but innocent and pure;
No sovereignty —

SEBASTIAN   Yet he would be king on't. 155

ANTONIO   The latter end of his commonwealth forgets the
beginning.

GONZALO   All things in common nature should produce
Without sweat or endeavour. Treason, felony,
Sword, pike, knife, gun, or need of any engine, 160
Would I not have, but nature should bring forth,
Of it own kind, all foison, all abundance,
To feed my innocent people.

SEBASTIAN   No marrying 'mong his subjects?

ANTONIO   None, man. All idle, whores and knaves. 165

GONZALO   I would with such perfection govern, sir,
T' excel the golden age.

SEBASTIAN   Save his Majesty!

ANTONIO   Long live Gonzalo!

GONZALO   And — do you mark me, sir?

ALONSO   Prithee, no more. Thou dost talk nothing to me. 170

GONZALO   I do well believe your Highness, and did it to
minister occasion to these gentlemen, who are of such
sensible and nimble lungs that they always use to laugh
at nothing.

ANTONIO   'Twas you we laughed at. 175

GONZALO   Who in this kind of merry fooling am nothing to
you. So you may continue, and laugh at nothing still.

ANTONIO   What a blow was there given!

SEBASTIAN   An it had not fall'n flat-long.

Act 2, Scene 1

GONZALO   You are gentlemen of brave mettle. You would   180
lift the moon out of her sphere, if she would continue in
it five weeks without changing.

180-182 'You're such bold fellows. You'd pull the moon down out of the sky if it went five weeks without changing.'

Enter ARIEL, *invisible, playing solemn music*

bat-fowling = bat-hunting

SEBASTIAN   We would so, and then go a-bat-fowling.

ANTONIO   Nay, good my lord, be not angry.

GONZALO   No, I warrant you — I will not adventure my   185
discretion so weakly. Will you laugh me asleep, for I am
very heavy?

185-187 'It's all right — I promise not to show you my true feelings. Why don't you laugh me to sleep? I'm very tired.'

ANTONIO   Go sleep, and hear us.

All sleep but ALONSO, SEBASTIAN *and* ANTONIO

ALONSO   What, all so soon asleep! I wish mine eyes
Would, with themselves, shut up my thoughts. I find   190
They are inclined to do so.

189-191 'I wish I could go to sleep and forget my troubles. Actually, I am a bit sleepy.'

SEBASTIAN   Please you, sir,
Do not omit the heavy offer of it.
It seldom visits sorrow — when it doth,
It is a comforter.

192-194 'Have a nap then. It's hard to sleep when you're upset — if you can it does you good.'

ANTONIO   We two, my lord,
Will guard your person while you take your rest,   195
And watch your safety.

ALONSO   Thank you — wondrous heavy!

ALONSO *sleeps. Exit* ARIEL.

SEBASTIAN   What a strange drowsiness possesses them!

ANTONIO   It is the quality o' th' climate.

198 'It's the weather on this island that makes them sleepy.'

SEBASTIAN   Why
Doth it not then our eyelids sink? I find not
Myself disposed to sleep.

198-200 'Why aren't we tired then? I don't feel sleepy?'

ANTONIO   Nor I. My spirits are nimble.   200
They fell together all, as by consent —
They dropped, as by a thunder-stroke. What might,
Worthy Sebastian — O, what might! No more!
And yet methinks I see it in thy face,
What thou shouldst be. Th' occasion speaks thee, and   205
My strong imagination sees a crown
Dropping upon thy head.

202-207 'Good old Sebastian... you could... I'd better not say! But I can see you've got so much potential. I think your time has come, and you could end up King.'

SEBASTIAN   What, art thou waking?

ANTONIO   Do you not hear me speak?

SEBASTIAN   I do, and surely
It is a sleepy language, and thou speak'st
Out of thy sleep. What is it thou didst say?   210
This is a strange repose, to be asleep
With eyes wide open, standing, speaking, moving,
And yet so fast asleep.

208-213 'You're only saying things like that because you're tired. What did you say? This is very odd — your eyes are open, you're standing, speaking and moving but sound asleep.'

ANTONIO   Noble Sebastian,
Thou let'st thy fortune sleep — die rather. Wink'st
Whiles thou art waking.

214-215 'You're missing a big chance. You're walking around with your eyes closed.'

SEBASTIAN   Thou dost snore distinctly,   215
There's meaning in thy snores.

215 'You're snoring very clearly'

217-219 'I'm being serious for once. Stop joking and listen to me and you'll find yourself three times better off.'

ANTONIO I am more serious than my custom. You
Must be so too, if heed me, which to do
Trebles thee o'er.

219 'I'm being quiet now.'

SEBASTIAN Well, I am standing water.

flow = take action

ANTONIO I'll teach you how to flow.

SEBASTIAN Do so: to ebb, 220

220-221 'I'm naturally a slacker.'

Hereditary sloth instructs me.

ANTONIO O,

222-226 'You're taking the mickey and that just proves how much you want to do this! You're pretending you don't care but really you do! Most men without much power only live like that because they're frightened or lazy.'

If you but knew how you the purpose cherish,
Whiles thus you mock it! How, in stripping it,
You more invest it! Ebbing men indeed,
Most often, do so near the bottom run 225
By their own fear or sloth.

SEBASTIAN Prithee say on.
The setting of thine eye and cheek proclaim

prithee = I beg you
227-229 'You look like you're about to come out with something interesting, and something that's quite hard to say.'

A matter from thee, and a birth, indeed,
Which throes thee much to yield.

ANTONIO Thus, sir:

230-236 'Old Gonzalo here, a forgetful man who'll quickly be forgotten when he's dead, has nearly persuaded Alonso that Ferdinand's alive, but I think that's very unlikely.'

Although this lord of weak remembrance, this 230
Who shall be of as little memory
When he is earthed, hath here almost persuaded —
For he's a spirit of persuasion, only
Professes to persuade — the King his son's alive,
'Tis as impossible that he's undrowned 235
As he that sleeps here swims.

SEBASTIAN I have no hope
That he's undrowned.

237-241 '"No hope" for Ferdinand means great hopes for you! It means such high hopes that you couldn't really aim any higher.'

ANTONIO O, out of that 'no hope'
What great hope have you! No hope that way is
Another way so high a hope, that even
Ambition cannot pierce a wink beyond, 240
But doubt discovery there. Will you grant with me
That Ferdinand is drowned?

SEBASTIAN He's gone.

ANTONIO Then tell me,
Who's the next heir of Naples?

SEBASTIAN Claribel.

244-252 'She lives miles from anywhere. It would take years to send her a message, as long as it would take a boy who's a baby now to start shaving. She's the reason we were shipwrecked, and now it's your destiny and mine to take control of our future.'

ANTONIO She that is Queen of Tunis, she that dwells
Ten leagues beyond man's life, she that from Naples 245
Can have no note — unless the sun were post,
The Man i' th' Moon's too slow — till newborn chins
Be rough and razorable; she that from whom
We all were sea-swallowed, though some cast again,
And by that destiny, to perform an act 250
Whereof what's past is prologue, what to come
In yours and my discharge.

SEBASTIAN What stuff is this! How say you?
'Tis true, my brother's daughter's Queen of Tunis.
So is she heir of Naples, 'twixt which regions 255
There is some space.

'twixt = between

ANTONIO   A space whose ev'ry cubit
    Seems to cry out 'How shall that Claribel
    Measure us back to Naples? Keep in Tunis,
    And let Sebastian wake.' Say this were death
    That now hath seized them, why, they were no worse   260
    Than now they are. There be that can rule Naples
    As well as he that sleeps, lords that can prate
    As amply and unnecessarily
    As this Gonzalo. I myself could make
    A chough of as deep chat. O, that you bore   265
    The mind that I do! What a sleep were this
    For your advancement! Do you understand me?

SEBASTIAN   Methinks I do.

ANTONIO   And how does your content
    Tender your own good fortune?

SEBASTIAN   I remember
    You did supplant your brother Prospero.

ANTONIO   True.   270
    And look how well my garments sit upon me,
    Much feater than before. My brother's servants
    Were then my fellows, now they are my men.

SEBASTIAN   But, for your conscience —

ANTONIO   Ay, sir, where lies that? If 'twere a kibe,   275
    'Twould put me to my slipper, but I feel not
    This deity in my bosom. Twenty consciences
    That stand 'twixt me and Milan, candied be they
    And melt, ere they molest! Here lies your brother,
    No better than the earth he lies upon,   280
    If he were that which now he's like — that's dead —
    Whom I with this obedient steel, three inches of it,
    Can lay to bed for ever, whiles you, doing thus,
    To the perpetual wink for aye might put
    This ancient morsel, this Sir Prudence, who   285
    Should not upbraid our course. For all the rest,
    They'll take suggestion as a cat laps milk,
    They'll tell the clock to any business that
    We say befits the hour.

SEBASTIAN   Thy case, dear friend,
    Shall be my precedent. As thou got'st Milan,   290
    I'll come by Naples. Draw thy sword. One stroke
    Shall free thee from the tribute which thou payest,
    And I the King shall love thee.

ANTONIO   Draw together,
    And when I rear my hand, do you the like,
    To fall it on Gonzalo.

SEBASTIAN   O, but one word — (they talk apart)   295

        Re-enter ARIEL, invisible, with music and song

ARIEL   My master through his art foresees the danger
    That you, his friend, are in, and sends me forth —
    For else his project dies — to keep them living.

        (sings in GONZALO's ear)

cubit = the length of a forearm, about 30cm

257-267 '"How's Claribel going to make it back to Naples? She should stay in Tunis and let Sebastian stir himself to action." If Alonso and Gonzalo were lying here dead they wouldn't be any worse off than they are now. There are others who could rule Naples as well as Alonso, and others who can babble on like Gonzalo. I could do his job. I wish you thought like me! This is such a big opportunity!'

chough = noisy black bird

268-269 'If you like my plan, what are you going to do about it?'

supplant = take over from

garments = royal robes

feater = fitting more neatly

fellows = equals

275-279 'What conscience? If it was a physical pain, like a chilblain, I'd do something about it, but as it is I don't feel a thing. If there were twenty consciences trying to stop me from being Duke of Milan, I'd let them be sugared and melted before I let them bother me!'

281-289 'He's sleeping like a dead man, and I can put him out of the way forever with my trusty dagger here, while you finish off old Gonzalo so he can't moan on about what we've done. There's no need to worry about the others. They'll do whatever we say.'

289-292 'I'll follow your example and become King of Naples the same way you became Duke of Milan. Draw your sword. One blow will free you of the taxes you pay to Naples'

294-295 'When I raise my hand, you do the same and stab Gonzalo.'

While you here do snoring lie,
Open-eyed conspiracy   300
His time doth take.
If of life you keep a care,
Shake off slumber, and beware.
Awake, awake!

ANTONIO   Then let us both be sudden.   305

GONZALO   *(wakes)* Now, good angels preserve the King!

ALONSO   *(wakes)* Why, how now? Ho, awake! Why are you
                                                    drawn?

308 'What's that dreadful — Wherefore this ghastly looking?
face you're making?'

GONZALO   What's the matter?

*securing your repose = guarding
you while you were sleeping*

SEBASTIAN   Whiles we stood here securing your repose,
Even now, we heard a hollow burst of bellowing   310
Like bulls, or rather lions — did't not wake you?
It struck mine ear most terribly.

ALONSO   I heard nothing.

ANTONIO   O, 'twas a din to fright a monster's ear,
To make an earthquake! Sure it was the roar
Of a whole herd of lions.

ALONSO   Heard you this, Gonzalo?   315

verily = true

GONZALO   Upon mine honour, sir, I heard a humming,
And that a strange one too, which did awake me.
I shaked you, sir, and cried. As mine eyes opened,
I saw their weapons drawn — there was a noise,
That's verily. 'Tis best we stand upon our guard,   320
Or that we quit this place. Let's draw our weapons.

ALONSO   Lead off this ground; and let's make further search
For my poor son.

GONZALO   Heavens keep him from these beasts!
For he is, sure, i' th' island.

ALONSO   Lead away.

ARIEL   Prospero my lord shall know what I have done.   325
So, King, go safely on to seek thy son.

Exeunt

ACT 2 SCENE 2
Another part of the island

Enter CALIBAN, with a burden of wood.
A noise of thunder heard.

CALIBAN   All the infections that the sun sucks up
From bogs, fens, flats, on Prosper fall, and make him
By inch-meal a disease! His spirits hear me,
And yet I needs must curse. But they'll nor pinch,
Fright me with urchin-shows, pitch me i' th' mire,   5
Nor lead me, like a firebrand, in the dark
Out of my way, unless he bid 'em. But
For every trifle are they set upon me:
Sometime like apes that mow and chatter at me,
And after bite me; then like hedgehogs which   10
Lie tumbling in my barefoot way, and mount
Their pricks at my footfall; sometime am I
All wound with adders, who with cloven tongues
Do hiss me into madness.

Enter TRINCULO

                Lo, now, lo!
Here comes a spirit of his, and to torment me   15
For bringing wood in slowly. I'll fall flat —
Perchance he will not mind me.

TRINCULO   Here's neither bush nor shrub to bear off any
weather at all, and another storm brewing. I hear it sing
i' th' wind. Yond same black cloud, yond huge one,   20
looks like a foul bombard that would shed his liquor. If it
should thunder as it did before, I know not where to hide
my head. Yond same cloud cannot choose but fall by
pailfuls. What have we here? A man or a fish? Dead or
alive? A fish — he smells like a fish — a very ancient   25
and fish-like smell — kind of not-of-the-newest Poor-
John. A strange fish! Were I in England now, as once I
was, and had but this fish painted, not a holiday fool
there but would give a piece of silver. There would this
monster make a man — any strange beast there makes   30
a man. When they will not give a doit to relieve a lame
beggar, they will lay out ten to see a dead Indian.
Legged like a man, and his fins like arms! Warm, o' my
troth! I do now let loose my opinion, hold it no longer —
this is no fish, but an islander, that hath lately suffered by   35
a thunderbolt. *(thunder)* Alas, the storm is come again!
My best way is to creep under his gaberdine, there is no
other shelter hereabout. Misery acquaints a man with
strange bed-fellows. I will here shroud till the dregs of
the storm be past.   40

Enter STEPHANO singing, a bottle in his hand

STEPHANO   *(sings)* I shall no more to sea, to sea,
Here shall I die ashore —
This is a very scurvy tune to sing at a man's funeral.
Well, here's my comfort. *(drinks and sings)*

Caliban sees Trinculo and thinks he's one of Prospero's spirits come to punish him. Trinculo sees a storm coming and hides under Caliban's coat. Stephano finds them both and shares out his wine. Caliban loves the wine and offers to be Stephano's servant.

By inch-meal = every inch

3-7 'His spirits hear me but I can't stop myself from cursing. They don't pinch me, or scare me with illusions, or throw me in the swamp, or lead me astray with flaming torches in the darkness unless he commands it.'

mow = make faces

cloven = forked

14-17 'Uh-oh! Here comes one of his spirits to punish me for being slow with the firewood. I'll lie down flat and maybe he won't spot me.'

bear off = keep off

20-21 'That big black cloud looks like a rotten wine bottle, ready to dump its load.'

Poor-John = dried, salted fish (very smelly)

27-32 'If I was in England, I could make a fortune by using this weirdo in a freak-show. They'll pay loads for odd balls like him there.'

33-36 'I swear he's alive! I'm going to say what I think, no holding back — this isn't a fish, it's an islander who's been struck by lightning.'

37-40 'There's no other shelter here, I'll creep under his coat. Hard times make for unusual situations. I'll hide here till the storm's over.'

scurvy = rotten, diseased

master = ship's owner

swabber = sailor who mops the decks

boatswain = second-in-command

The master, the swabber, the boatswain, and I, 45
The gunner, and his mate,
Loved Mall, Meg, and Marian, and Margery,
But none of us cared for Kate,
For she had a tongue with a tang,
Would cry to a sailor 'Go hang!' 50
She loved not the savour of tar nor of pitch,
Yet a tailor might scratch her where'er she did itch.
Then to sea, boys, and let her go hang!
This is a scurvy tune too, but here's my comfort. *(drinks)*

CALIBAN Do not torment me. O! 55

56-61 'Are you playing tricks on us with savages and Indians? Ha! I didn't escape drowning just to be afraid of you and your four legs. As the saying goes, 'He won't give way to any man that walks on four legs,' and it'll be said again so long as I'm alive.'

STEPHANO What's the matter? Have we devils here? Do you put tricks upon's with savages and men of Ind? Ha! I have not scaped drowning to be afeard now of your four legs, for it hath been said, 'As proper a man as ever went on four legs cannot make him give ground,' and it shall 60 be said so again, while Stephano breathes at nostrils.

CALIBAN The spirit torments me. O!

ague = fever

STEPHANO This is some monster of the isle with four legs, who hath got, as I take it, an ague. Where the devil should he learn our language? I will give him some 65 relief, if it be but for that. If I can recover him, and keep him tame, and get to Naples with him, he's a present for any emperor that ever trod on neat's leather.

65-68 'He speaks my language so I'll ease his pain a bit. If I capture and tame him and take him back to Naples, he'll make a great present for any emperor who wears shoes.'

CALIBAN Do not torment me, prithee — I'll bring my wood home faster. 70

71-76 'He's having a fit and not making much sense. I'll let him have a drink — if he's never had wine before it'll cure the fit. If I capture and tame him I won't sell him for much. Whoever wants him will pay well enough.'

STEPHANO He's in his fit now, and does not talk after the wisest. He shall taste of my bottle — if he have never drunk wine afore, it will go near to remove his fit. If I can recover him, and keep him tame, I will not take too much for him. He shall pay for him that hath him, and that 75 soundly.

77-79 'You're not hurting me yet, but I can tell you're about to. You're shaking and that means Prospero's doing his magic on you.'

CALIBAN Thou dost me yet but little hurt. Thou wilt anon, I know it by thy trembling — now Prosper works upon thee.

STEPHANO Come on your ways, open your mouth. Here 80 is that which will give language to you, cat. Open your mouth — this will shake your shaking, I can tell you, and that soundly. You cannot tell who's your friend. Open your chaps again.

chaps = jaws

85-86 'That's a familiar voice — it's... no it's not. He's drowned and these are devils.'

TRINCULO I should know that voice — it should be — but 85 he is drowned, and these are devils. O, defend me!

delicate = lovely

88-91 'His front voice speaks nicely to me, his back voice swears and moans. I'll give him all the wine in my bottle if it will cure him.'

STEPHANO Four legs and two voices; a most delicate monster! His forward voice, now, is to speak well of his friend, his backward voice is to utter foul speeches and to detract. If all the wine in my bottle will recover him, I 90 will help his ague. Come — Amen! I will pour some in thy other mouth.

TRINCULO Stephano!

STEPHANO Doth thy other mouth call me? Mercy, mercy! This is a devil, and no monster. I will leave him, I have no 95 long spoon.

95-96 There was a proverb that said 'You need a long spoon to eat with the devil.'

TRINCULO Stephano! If thou be'st Stephano, touch me, and speak to me, for I am Trinculo — be not afeard — thy good friend Trinculo.

STEPHANO If thou be'st Trinculo, come forth. I'll pull thee **100** by the lesser legs — if any be Trinculo's legs, these are they. *(Pulls him from under the cloak)* Thou art very Trinculo indeed! How cam'st thou to be the siege of this mooncalf? Can he vent Trinculos?

TRINCULO I took him to be killed with a thunderstroke. But **105** art thou not drowned, Stephano? I hope now thou are not drowned. Is the storm overblown? I hid me under the dead mooncalf's gaberdine for fear of the storm. And art thou living, Stephano? O Stephano, two Neapolitans scaped! **110**

STEPHANO Prithee, do not turn me about — my stomach is not constant.

CALIBAN *(aside)* These be fine things, an if they be not sprites.
That's a brave god, and bears celestial liquor.
I will kneel to him. **115**

STEPHANO How didst thou scape? How cam'st thou hither? Swear by this bottle how thou cam'st hither — I escaped upon a butt of sack, which the sailors heaved o'erboard — by this bottle, which I made of the bark of a tree, with mine own hands, since I was cast ashore. **120**

CALIBAN I'll swear upon that bottle to be thy true subject, for the liquor is not earthly.

STEPHANO Here, swear then how thou escapedst.

TRINCULO Swum ashore, man, like a duck. I can swim like a duck, I'll be sworn. **125**

STEPHANO *(passing the bottle)* Here, kiss the book. Though thou canst swim like a duck, thou art made like a goose.

TRINCULO O Stephano, hast any more of this?

STEPHANO The whole butt, man. My cellar is in a rock by **130** th' seaside, where my wine is hid. How now, mooncalf! How does thine ague?

CALIBAN Hast thou not dropped from heaven?

STEPHANO Out o' th' moon, I do assure thee. I was the Man i' th' Moon, when time was. **135**

CALIBAN I have seen thee in her, and I do adore thee. My mistress showed me thee, and thy dog and thy bush.

STEPHANO Come, swear to that — kiss the book. I will furnish it anon with new contents. Swear.

CALIBAN *drinks*

TRINCULO By this good light, this is a very shallow **140** monster! I afeard of him! A very weak monster! The Man i' th' Moon! A most poor credulous monster! Well drawn, monster, in good sooth!

CALIBAN I'll show thee every fertile inch o' th' island and I

103-104 'How did you end up being this deformed thing's droppings? Can he poo Trinculos?'

I took him = I believed he was

gaberdine = cloak

scaped = escaped

111-112 'Please don't spin me round like that — I'm feeling queasy.'

113-115 'If these aren't spirits they're fine creatures. The one with the heavenly drink is a great god. I'll worship him.'

116-120 'How did you get here? Swear on the bottle and tell me. I escaped by holding onto a barrel of wine which the sailors threw overboard. Swear on this bottle which I made from tree bark after I was washed up on the island.'

126 "Kissing the book" meant swearing an oath by kissing the Bible.

butt = cask of wine

135, 137 The Man in the Moon was thought to be a man who collected firewood on a Sunday and was sent to the moon as a punishment. His dog and a bush were sent with him.

138-139 'I'll fill it up again straightaway.'

shallow = feeble-minded

142-143 'Poor monster, you're so easily fooled! That was a good gulp!'

Act 2, Scene 2

perfidious = *scheming*

in drink = *drunk*

158-159 'Curses on Prospero! I won't carry sticks for him anymore'

161-162 'What a ridiculous creature to be so impressed by a drunk!'

crabs = *crab apples*

pig-nuts = *tasty roots*

snare = *trap*

filberts = *hazelnuts*

168 Nobody really knows what these are, but it's probably some sort of shellfish.

170-172 'Trinculo, the King and everyone else are dead, so we're in charge now. You carry the bottle. Trinculo, my friend, we'll fill it up again soon.'

trenchering = *plates*

will kiss thy foot. I prithee be my god.   145

TRINCULO By this light, a most perfidious and drunken
    monster! When's god's asleep he'll rob his bottle.

CALIBAN I'll kiss thy foot. I'll swear myself thy subject.

STEPHANO Come on, then — down, and swear.

TRINCULO I shall laugh myself to death at this puppy-   150
    headed monster. A most scurvy monster! I could find in
    my heart to beat him —

STEPHANO Come, kiss.

TRINCULO — but that the poor monster's in drink. An
    abominable monster!   155

CALIBAN I'll show thee the best springs. I'll pluck thee
                           berries.
    I'll fish for thee, and get thee wood enough.
    A plague upon the tyrant that I serve!
    I'll bear him no more sticks, but follow thee,
    Thou wondrous man.   160

TRINCULO A most ridiculous monster, to make a wonder of
    a poor drunkard!

CALIBAN I prithee let me bring thee where crabs grow,
    And I with my long nails will dig thee pig-nuts,
    Show thee a jay's nest, and instruct thee how   165
    To snare the nimble marmoset. I'll bring thee
    To clust'ring filberts, and sometimes I'll get thee
    Young scamels from the rock. Wilt thou go with me?

STEPHANO I prithee now, lead the way without any more
    talking. Trinculo, the King and all our company else   170
    being drowned, we will inherit here. Here, bear my
    bottle. Fellow Trinculo, we'll fill him by and by again.

CALIBAN *(sings drunkenly)* Farewell, master! Farewell,
    farewell!

TRINCULO A howling monster, a drunken monster!   175

CALIBAN No more dams I'll make for fish;
    Nor fetch in firing at requiring,
    Nor scrape trenchering, nor wash dish.
    'Ban 'Ban, Ca-Caliban,
    Has a new master, get a new man.   180
    Freedom, high-day! High-day, freedom! Freedom,
                          high-day, freedom!

STEPHANO O brave monster! Lead the way.

Exeunt

Act 2 — Revision Summary

Shakespeare must have liked Act 1 because he carried on and wrote another one. And seemingly he was fairly chuffed with Act 2 because there are three more to go after this one. Have a lovely refreshing break before you get stuck into Act 3. Make a cup of tea. Go and stand by the window to get some fresh air. Breathe in. Breathe out. Breathe in. Breathe out. Right, that's enough. Now come back over here and answer these tasty questions.

SCENE 1

1) List all the characters who appear in this scene.
2) What not-very-good reason does Gonzalo give for being happy?
3) Who teases Gonzalo and Adrian?
4) What odd thing does Gonzalo notice about everyone's clothes?
5) Who's Claribel? What has she done in Tunis?
6) Who's Dido? What happened to her?
7) What's Alonso so upset about?
8) What news does Francisco have, that should cheer Alonso up?
9) Does it work?
10) Why does Sebastian think everything that's happened is Alonso's fault?
11) In lines 146-167 Gonzalo explains how he'd run the island if it was his. Describe his ideal kingdom in your own words.
12) Who goes to sleep? What happens to make them nod off?
13) Who stays awake?
14) What does Antonio suggest to Sebastian?
15) Does Sebastian agree straightaway, or does Antonio have to persuade him?
16) What stops Sebastian and Antonio from going through with their plan?
17) What reason do they give for having drawn their swords?
18) What do the characters go off to do at the end of the scene?

SCENE 2

19) What's Caliban carrying at the beginning of the scene?
20) Caliban can't stop himself from cursing Prospero. Why might it be better if he did stop?
21) What does "mow" mean in line 9?
22) Who's Trinculo? (Look at the inside front cover for a reminder if you need to.)
23) Why is Caliban scared of Trinculo?
24) Trinculo's worried that the weather might turn nasty again. Write down any phrase from his first speech that describes the weather.
25) What does he do to shelter from the weather?
26) What's Stephano's "comfort"?
27) Why does Stephano think Caliban has four legs?
28) How did Stephano escape from the shipwreck?
29) How did Trinculo escape from the shipwreck?
30) List five things that Caliban says he'll do for Stephano.

Miranda feels sorry for Ferdinand, who's lugging logs for Prospero. Ferdinand doesn't mind so long as he can see his lovely Miranda. Prospero watches secretly — he's really happy the two young 'uns are in love.

ACT 3 SCENE 1
Before Prospero's cell

Enter FERDINAND, *bearing a log*

1-7 *'There are some sports which are hard work, but the fun you have makes up for it. You can put up with some humiliation. Most difficult situations lead to something better. Normally I'd hate what I'm doing but knowing I'm helping Miranda makes it OK.'*

crabbed = sour, bitter

9-15 *'I'm under strict instructions to pile up thousands of these logs. It makes her cry to see me work. She says nobody like me has ever had to put up with this humiliation before. I forget... These sweet thoughts make me feel better about my work even as I'm doing it.'*

22 *'before I've finished'*
strive = struggle

FERDINAND   There be some sports are painful, and their labour
Delight in them sets off, some kinds of baseness
Are nobly undergone, and most poor matters
Point to rich ends. This my mean task
Would be as heavy to me as odious, but   5
The mistress which I serve quickens what's dead,
And makes my labours pleasures. O, she is
Ten times more gentle than her father's crabbed,
And he's composed of harshness. I must remove
Some thousands of these logs, and pile them up,   10
Upon a sore injunction. My sweet mistress
Weeps when she sees me work, and says such baseness
Had never like executor. I forget —
But these sweet thoughts do even refresh my labours
Most busiest when I do it.

Enter MIRANDA, *and* PROSPERO *at a distance, unseen*

MIRANDA   Alas, now, pray you,   15
Work not so hard. I would the lightning had
Burnt up those logs that you are enjoined to pile.
Pray, set it down and rest you. When this burns,
'Twill weep for having wearied you. My father
Is hard at study. Pray, now, rest yourself,   20
He's safe for these three hours.

FERDINAND   O most dear mistress,
The sun will set before I shall discharge
What I must strive to do.

MIRANDA   If you'll sit down,
I'll bear your logs the while. Pray give me that,
I'll carry it to the pile.

FERDINAND   No, precious creature —   25
I had rather crack my sinews, break my back,
Than you should such dishonour undergo,
While I sit lazy by.

28-31 *'It's no more dishonourable for me than it is for you, and it would be easier for me, because my heart would be in the work and yours isn't.'*

31-32 *'Poor thing, you've caught the lovebug. The symptoms prove it.'*

33-34 *'even night feels like morning when you're with me'*

your hest = my promise to you

MIRANDA   It would become me
As well as it does you, and I should do it
With much more ease, for my good will is to it,   30
And yours it is against.

PROSPERO *(aside)*   Poor worm, thou art infected!
This visitation shows it.

MIRANDA   You look wearily.

FERDINAND   No, noble mistress — 'tis fresh morning with me
When you are by at night. I do beseech you,
Chiefly that I might set it in my prayers,   35
What is your name?

MIRANDA   Miranda — O my father,
I have broke your hest to say so!

FERDINAND   Admired Miranda!
Indeed the top of admiration, worth

What's dearest to the world! Full many a lady
I have eyed with best regard, and many a time   40
Th' harmony of their tongues hath into bondage
Brought my too diligent ear. For several virtues
Have I liked several women, never any
With so full soul, but some defect in her
Did quarrel with the noblest grace she owed,   45
And put it to the foil — but you, O you,
So perfect and so peerless, are created
Of every creature's best!

MIRANDA   I do not know
One of my sex, no woman's face remember,
Save, from my glass, mine own, nor have I seen   50
More that I may call men than you, good friend,
And my dear father. How features are abroad,
I am skilless of, but, by my modesty,
The jewel in my dower, I would not wish
Any companion in the world but you,   55
Nor can imagination form a shape,
Besides yourself, to like of. But I prattle
Something too wildly, and my father's precepts
I therein do forget.

FERDINAND   I am, in my condition,
A prince, Miranda. I do think, a king —   60
I would not so — and would no more endure
This wooden slavery than to suffer
The flesh-fly blow my mouth! Hear my soul speak:
The very instant that I saw you, did
My heart fly to your service, there resides   65
To make me slave to it, and for your sake
Am I this patient log-man.

MIRANDA   Do you love me?

FERDINAND O heaven, O earth, bear witness to this sound,
And crown what I profess with kind event,
If I speak true! If hollowly, invert   70
What best is boded me to mischief! I,
Beyond all limit of what else i' th' world,
Do love, prize, honour you.

MIRANDA   I am a fool
To weep at what I am glad of.

PROSPERO (aside)   Fair encounter
Of two most rare affections! Heavens rain grace   75
On that which breeds between 'em!

FERDINAND   Wherefore weep you?

MIRANDA At mine unworthiness, that dare not offer
What I desire to give, and much less take
What I shall die to want. But this is trifling,
And all the more it seeks to hide itself,   80
The bigger bulk it shows. Hence, bashful cunning,
And prompt me, plain and holy innocence!
I am your wife, if you will marry me,
If not, I'll die your maid. To be your fellow
You may deny me, but I'll be your servant,   85

39-48 'I've had my eye on lots of ladies in the past, and often their sweet words have drawn me in. I've never completely fallen for any of them because they always had some fault. But you're perfect!'

peerless = incomparable

NUMBER 1

glass = mirror

52-59 'I've got no idea what people look like in the rest of the world, but (I swear on my virginity) you're the one for me. I can't even imagine anyone better. But I'm prattling on, and my dad told me not to.'

precepts = rules

59-63 'I'm a Prince, Miranda. I think I'm a King, though I wish I wasn't. I'd rather blowflies laid eggs in my mouth than put up with this wood-lugging slavery!'

64-67 'I was your slave from the moment I saw you, and I can put up with all this for your sake.'

68-73 'Listen to me, heaven and earth, and reward me if I'm telling the truth! If I'm lying turn everything good that could happen to me to bad! I love you more than anything in the world.'

74-76 'They're perfect for each other! All the best to them!'

wherefore = why

77-86 'I'm not worthy of you. I don't dare to say I'm in love with you or ask if you're in love with me. But this is silly. The more I try not to say it the more obvious it is. Enough mucking about! I'll be your wife if you'll marry me. If not I'll never marry anyone else. You can refuse to have me as your wife, but I'll be your servant whether you like it or not.'

Act 3, Scene 1

Whether you will or no.

FERDINAND   My mistress, dearest,
And I thus humble ever.

MIRANDA   My husband, then?

FERDINAND   Ay, with a heart as willing
As bondage e'er of freedom. Here's my hand.

MIRANDA   And mine, with my heart in't. And now farewell   90
Till half an hour hence.

FERDINAND   A thousand thousand!

Exeunt FERDINAND *and* MIRANDA *separately*

PROSPERO   So glad of this as they I cannot be,
Who are surprised withal, but my rejoicing
At nothing can be more. I'll to my book,
For yet ere supper time must I perform   95
Much business appertaining.

Exit

86-87 'You'll be my wife, and I'll obey you.'

88-89 'As gladly as a prisoner is glad to be freed.'

hence = from now

A thousand thousand = a million goodbyes

92-96 'I can't be as happy as them because all this is no surprise to me, but I'm still chuffed to bits. I'll go and look at my books — there's a lot to do before supper time.'

appertaining = connected to this

Act 3, Scene 1

ACT 3 SCENE 2
Another part of the island

Enter CALIBAN, STEPHANO, and TRINCULO

Caliban, Stephano and Trinculo have been drinking constantly and they're all drunk. Caliban persuades Stephano to kill Prospero and make himself king of the island.

STEPHANO Tell not me — when the butt is out we will drink water, not a drop before. Therefore bear up, and board 'em. Servant-monster, drink to me.

when the butt is out = when we've run out of wine

board 'em = get on board, join in

TRINCULO Servant-monster! The folly of this island! They say there's but five upon this isle: we are three of them. If th'other two be brained like us, the state totters. 5

folly = foolishness

6 'If the other two are as drunk as us, this place is on the point of collapse.'

STEPHANO Drink, servant-monster, when I bid thee — thy eyes are almost set in thy head.

bid = order

7-8 'you're almost entirely sozzled'

TRINCULO Where should they be set else? He were a brave monster indeed, if they were set in his tail. 10

STEPHANO My man-monster hath drowned his tongue in sack. For my part, the sea cannot drown me. I swam, ere I could recover the shore, five and thirty leagues, off and on. By this light, thou shalt be my lieutenant, monster, or my standard. 15

11-12 'My monster's had so much wine he can't speak.'

TRINCULO Your lieutenant, if you list. He's no standard.

standard = the symbol on my banner

STEPHANO We'll not run, Monsieur Monster.

TRINCULO Nor go neither, but you'll lie like dogs, and yet say nothing neither.

STEPHANO Mooncalf, speak once in thy life, if thou be'st a good mooncalf. 20

CALIBAN How does thy honour? Let me lick thy shoe. I'll not serve him — he is not valiant.

22 'How are you, your honour?'

TRINCULO Thou liest, most ignorant monster: I am in case to jostle a constable. Why, thou deboshed fish, thou, 25 was there ever man a coward that hath drunk so much sack as I today? Wilt thou tell a monstrous lie, being but half a fish and half a monster?

24-27 'You're lying. I'm ready to fight a constable. You drunken fish, can anyone who's drunk as much wine as I have today be called a coward?'

CALIBAN Lo, how he mocks me! Wilt thou let him, my lord? 30

TRINCULO 'Lord' quoth he! That a monster should be such a natural!

natural = fool, idiot

CALIBAN Lo, lo again! Bite him to death, I prithee.

STEPHANO Trinculo, keep a good tongue in your head. If you prove a mutineer — the next tree! The poor 35 monster's my subject, and he shall not suffer indignity.

34-36 'Trinculo, don't be rude. If you rebel I'll hang you! He's my monster and I want him treated properly.'

CALIBAN I thank my noble lord. Wilt thou be pleased to hearken once again to the suit I made to thee?

37-38 'Shall I tell you my plan again?'

STEPHANO Marry will I — kneel and repeat it. I will stand, and so shall Trinculo. 40

marry = definitely

Enter ARIEL, invisible

CALIBAN As I told thee before, I am subject to a tyrant, A sorcerer, that by his cunning hath Cheated me of the Island.

ARIEL *(in TRINCULO's voice)* Thou liest.

44 Ariel tries to make the troublemakers fall out by imitating Trinculo arguing with Caliban.

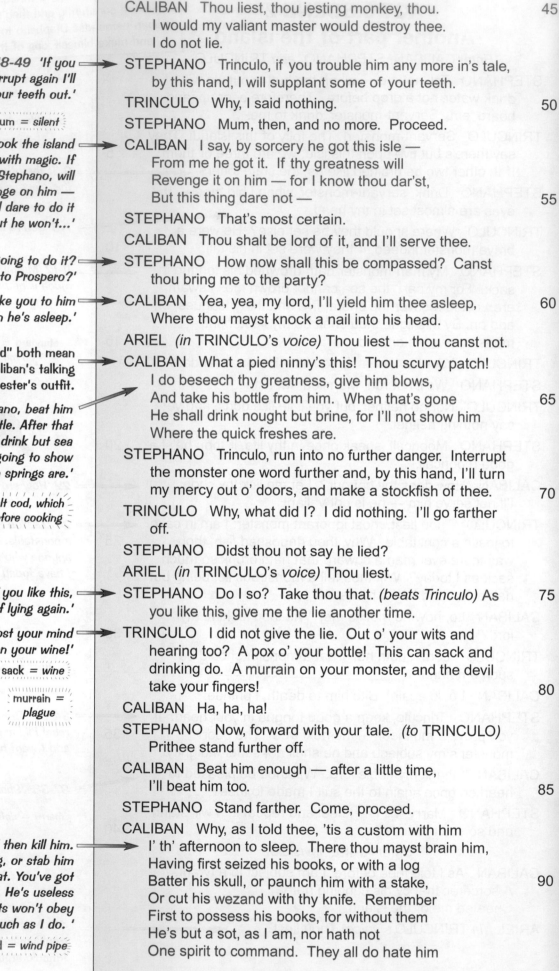

48-49 'If you interrupt again I'll knock your teeth out.'

Mum = silent

52-55 'He took the island away from me with magic. If you, great Stephano, will take your revenge on him — I know you will dare to do it but he won't...'

58-59 'How are we going to do it? Can you take me to Prospero?'

60 'I'll take you to him when he's asleep.'

63 "Pied" and "patched" both mean multi-coloured. Caliban's talking about Trinculo's jester's outfit.

64-67 'I beg you, Stephano, beat him and take away his bottle. After that he'll have nothing to drink but sea water, because I'm not going to show him where the fresh springs are.'

stockfish = salt cod, which was beaten before cooking

75-76 'If you like this, accuse me of lying again.'

77-78 'I didn't. You've lost your mind and your hearing. Curses on your wine!'

sack = wine

murrain = plague

88-95 'Take his books and then kill him. Smash his skull with a log, or stab him with a stake, or cut his throat. You've got to take the books first. He's useless without them and the spirits won't obey him. They all hate him as much as I do.'

wezand = wind pipe

CALIBAN   Thou liest, thou jesting monkey, thou.
           I would my valiant master would destroy thee.
           I do not lie.   45

STEPHANO   Trinculo, if you trouble him any more in's tale,
           by this hand, I will supplant some of your teeth.

TRINCULO   Why, I said nothing.   50

STEPHANO   Mum, then, and no more. Proceed.

CALIBAN   I say, by sorcery he got this isle —
           From me he got it. If thy greatness will
           Revenge it on him — for I know thou dar'st,
           But this thing dare not —   55

STEPHANO   That's most certain.

CALIBAN   Thou shalt be lord of it, and I'll serve thee.

STEPHANO   How now shall this be compassed? Canst
           thou bring me to the party?

CALIBAN   Yea, yea, my lord, I'll yield him thee asleep,   60
           Where thou mayst knock a nail into his head.

ARIEL   (in TRINCULO's voice) Thou liest — thou canst not.

CALIBAN   What a pied ninny's this! Thou scurvy patch!
           I do beseech thy greatness, give him blows,
           And take his bottle from him. When that's gone   65
           He shall drink nought but brine, for I'll not show him
           Where the quick freshes are.

STEPHANO   Trinculo, run into no further danger. Interrupt
           the monster one word further and, by this hand, I'll turn
           my mercy out o' doors, and make a stockfish of thee.   70

TRINCULO   Why, what did I? I did nothing. I'll go farther
           off.

STEPHANO   Didst thou not say he lied?

ARIEL   (in TRINCULO's voice) Thou liest.

STEPHANO   Do I so? Take thou that. (beats Trinculo) As   75
           you like this, give me the lie another time.

TRINCULO   I did not give the lie. Out o' your wits and
           hearing too? A pox o' your bottle! This can sack and
           drinking do. A murrain on your monster, and the devil
           take your fingers!   80

CALIBAN   Ha, ha, ha!

STEPHANO   Now, forward with your tale. (to TRINCULO)
           Prithee stand further off.

CALIBAN   Beat him enough — after a little time,
           I'll beat him too.   85

STEPHANO   Stand farther. Come, proceed.

CALIBAN   Why, as I told thee, 'tis a custom with him
           I' th' afternoon to sleep. There thou mayst brain him,
           Having first seized his books, or with a log
           Batter his skull, or paunch him with a stake,   90
           Or cut his wezand with thy knife. Remember
           First to possess his books, for without them
           He's but a sot, as I am, nor hath not
           One spirit to command. They all do hate him

As rootedly as I. Burn but his books.   95
He has brave utensils — for so he calls them —
Which, when he has a house, he'll deck withal.
And that most deeply to consider is
The beauty of his daughter — he himself
Calls her a nonpareil. I never saw a woman   100
But only Sycorax my dam and she,
But she as far surpasseth Sycorax
As great'st does least.

STEPHANO   Is it so brave a lass?

CALIBAN Ay, lord. She will become thy bed, I warrant,
And bring thee forth brave brood.   105

STEPHANO Monster, I will kill this man. His daughter and I
will be King and Queen — save our Graces! — and
Trinculo and thyself shall be viceroys. Dost thou like the
plot, Trinculo?

TRINCULO Excellent.   110

STEPHANO Give me thy hand — I am sorry I beat thee, but
while thou liv'st, keep a good tongue in thy head.

CALIBAN Within this half hour will he be asleep.
Wilt thou destroy him then?

STEPHANO   Ay, on mine honour.

ARIEL This will I tell my master.   115

CALIBAN Thou mak'st me merry. I am full of pleasure.
Let us be jocund — will you troll the catch
You taught me but whilere?

STEPHANO At thy request, monster, I will do reason, any
reason. Come on, Trinculo, let us sing.   120
(sings) Flout 'em and scout 'em,
And scout 'em and flout 'em;
Thought is free.

CALIBAN That's not the tune.

          ARIEL plays the tune on a tabor and pipe

STEPHANO What is this same?   125

TRINCULO This is the tune of our catch, played by the
picture of Nobody.

STEPHANO If thou be'st a man, show thyself in thy
likeness. If thou be'st a devil, take't as thou list.

TRINCULO O, forgive me my sins!   130

STEPHANO He that dies pays all debts. I defy thee. Mercy
upon us!

CALIBAN Art thou afeard?

STEPHANO No, monster, not I.

CALIBAN Be not afeard. The isle is full of noises,   135
Sounds, and sweet airs, that give delight, and hurt not.
Sometimes a thousand twangling instruments
Will hum about mine ears, and sometimes voices,
That, if I then had waked after long sleep,
Will make me sleep again, and then, in dreaming,   140
The clouds methought would open and show riches

95-103 'Burn his books but keep the furniture. And don't forget his daughter. She's gorgeous. I've never seen another woman except for my witch-mother Sycorax, but the daughter's way better-looking than her.'

104-105 'She'll look lovely in your bed, and produce a fine litter of children.'

viceroys = royal deputies

117-118 'Let's be cheery — will you sing that round you taught me earlier?'

tabor = drum

128-129 'If you're a man, show us what you look like. If you're a devil, do what you like.'

afeard = afraid

twangling = jingling

Act 3, Scene 2

Ready to drop upon me, that, when I waked,
I cried to dream again.

STEPHANO   This will prove a brave kingdom to me, where I
shall have my music for nothing.   145

144-145 'This is a great place to be king, if you can listen to music for free.'

CALIBAN   When Prospero is destroyed.

STEPHANO   That shall be by and by. I remember the story.

MP3 downloads FREE

taborer = drummers

TRINCULO   The sound is going away. Let's follow it, and
after do our work.

STEPHANO   Lead, monster — we'll follow. I would I could
see this taborer. He lays it on.   150

TRINCULO   Wilt come? I'll follow, Stephano.

Exeunt

Alonso, Gonzalo, Sebastian, Antonio and the others have been looking for Ferdinand. They stop for a break and spirits bring in a tasty-looking feast. They're just about to eat when Ariel comes in and tells them the shipwreck was their punishment for throwing Prospero out of Milan.

ACT 3 SCENE 3
Another part of the island
Enter ALONSO, SEBASTIAN, ANTONIO,
GONZALO, ADRIAN, FRANCISCO *and* OTHERS

by'r lakin = by our lady, by the Virgin Mary

GONZALO   By'r lakin, I can go no further, sir.
My old bones ache. Here's a maze trod, indeed,
Through forth-rights and meanders! By your patience,
I needs must rest me.

2-4 'We've been wandering about all over the place. I need a rest.'

ALONSO   Old lord, I cannot blame thee,
Who am myself attached with weariness   5
To th' dulling of my spirits. Sit down and rest.

4-6 'I don't blame you. I'm worn out too.'

Even here I will put off my hope, and keep it
No longer for my flatterer. He is drowned
Whom thus we stray to find, and the sea mocks
Our frustrate search on land. Well, let him go.   10

7-10 'As of now I'm giving up hope of finding Ferdinand. He's surely drowned, and the sea's laughing at us for searching the land.'

ANTONIO   *(aside to* SEBASTIAN*)* I am right glad that he's
                                                     so out of hope.

12-13 'I hope you haven't forgotten about our plan, just because it didn't work out first time round.'

Do not, for one repulse, forgo the purpose
That you resolved t' effect.

SEBASTIAN   *(aside to* ANTONIO*)* The next advantage
Will we take throughly.

13-14 'We'll make the most of the next chance we have.'

ANTONIO   *(aside to* SEBASTIAN*)* Let it be to-night,
For, now they are oppressed with travel, they   15
Will not, nor cannot, use such vigilance
As when they are fresh.

14-17 'Let's do it tonight. They're worn out from walking and it'll be easier to catch them off their guard.'

SEBASTIAN   *(aside to* ANTONIO*)* I say, to-night — no more.

Solemn and strange music; and PROSPERO *on the top, invisible. Enter several strange* SHAPES, *bringing in a banquet, and dance about it with gentle actions of salutations, and inviting the King etc. to eat, they depart.*

strange shapes = spirits

salutations = greetings

hark = listen

ALONSO   What harmony is this? My good friends, hark!

GONZALO   Marvellous sweet music!

ALONSO   Give us kind keepers, heavens! What were these?   20

kind keepers = guardian angels

SEBASTIAN   A living drollery. Now I will believe

drollery = puppet show

That there are unicorns, that in Arabia
There is one tree, the phoenix' throne, one phoenix
At this hour reigning there.

ANTONIO   I'll believe both,
And what does else want credit, come to me,   25
And I'll be sworn 'tis true. Travellers ne'er did lie,
Though fools at home condemn 'em.

GONZALO   If in Naples
I should report this now, would they believe me?
If I should say, I saw such islanders,
For certes these are people of the island,   30
Who though they are of monstrous shape, yet note,
Their manners are more gentle-kind than of
Our human generation you shall find
Many, nay, almost any.

PROSPERO (aside)   Honest lord,
Thou hast said well, for some of you there present   35
Are worse than devils.

ALONSO   I cannot too much muse
Such shapes, such gesture, and such sound, expressing,
Although they want the use of tongue, a kind
Of excellent dumb discourse.

PROSPERO (aside)   Praise in departing.

FRANCISCO They vanished strangely.

SEBASTIAN   No matter, since   40
They have left their viands behind, for we have stomachs.
Will't please you taste of what is here?

ALONSO   Not I.

GONZALO Faith, sir, you need not fear. When we were boys,
Who would believe that there were mountaineers,
Dewlapped like bulls, whose throats had hanging at 'em   45
Wallets of flesh? Or that there were such men
Whose heads stood in their breasts which now we find
Each putter-out of five for one will bring us
Good warrant of?

ALONSO   I will stand to, and feed,
Although my last. No matter, since I feel   50
The best is past. Brother, my lord the Duke,
Stand to, and do as we.

    Thunder and lightning. Enter ARIEL, like a harpy,
    claps his wings upon the table, and, with a
    quaint device, the banquet vanishes.

ARIEL You are three men of sin, whom Destiny,
That hath to instrument this lower world
And what is in't, the never-surfeited sea   55
Hath caused to belch up you, and on this island
Where man doth not inhabit — you 'mongst men
Being most unfit to live. I have made you mad,
And even with such-like valour men hang and drown
Their proper selves.

22-24 Arabian mythology said that the phoenix lived in the desert. Only one bird lived at a time. After 500 years it died and a new phoenix was born from the ashes of its funeral pyre.

31-34 'even though they're a funny shape, they've got better manners than most human beings'

36-39 'I'm totally amazed — by the shapes, the movements, the sounds. Even though they couldn't speak they got their message across.'

40-42 'It doesn't matter. They've left the food behind. Shall we eat it?'

43-49 'You don't need to be afraid, sir. When we were boys who would have believed that there are mountain-people with folds of flesh hanging from their necks like bulls? Or men with heads growing out of their chests, which everyone who goes on an expedition now swears they've seen?'

49-52 'I'll eat, even if this turns out to be my last meal. It doesn't matter now all my happiness is over. Come and join us Antonio and Sebastian.'

harpy = scary creature with wings, claws and a woman's head and body, sent by the Greek gods to punish wrong-doers

quaint device = cunning stage trick

53-60 'You three have all sinned. Destiny, which controls this world, has made the sea spit you up on this deserted island, even though you don't deserve to live. I've made you mad, and even the bravest men drown themselves through madness.'

Act 3, Scene 3

38

60-68 'We are servants of Fate. Your swords can do us as much harm as they could do the wind or the water. Even if you could do us any damage there's a spell on you to stop you lifting your swords.'

68-82 'This is my message to you — you three threw Prospero out of Milan, and cast him adrift on the sea with his innocent child. This storm and your shipwreck is your punishment from the powers above for those crimes. They've taken your son, Alonso, and you are condemned to a slow miserable death on this deserted island.'

with mocks and mows = making faces

83-93 'Nice performance Ariel. Stylish, and you remembered everything I asked you to say. The other spirits have done well too. My magic's working, and my enemies are completely bewildered. I'll leave them in their confusion while I go and see Ferdinand and Miranda.'

94-95 'What on earth are you staring at, sir?' Gonzalo didn't see any of Ariel's performance.

Prosperooooo...

96-102 'It seemed that the clouds spoke, the winds sang and thunder played a deep rumbling organ, all saying 'Prospero'. They named my crime and said that's why my son has drowned. I'll drown myself and join him at the bottom of the ocean.'

ALONSO, SEBASTIAN *etc. draw their swords*

You fools! I and my fellows   60
Are ministers of Fate, the elements
Of whom your swords are tempered may as well
Wound the loud winds, or with bemocked-at stabs
Kill the still-closing waters, as diminish
One dowl that's in my plume. My fellow-ministers 65
Are like invulnerable. If you could hurt,
Your swords are now too massy for your strengths
And will not be uplifted. But remember —
For that's my business to you — that you three
From Milan did supplant good Prospero,   70
Exposed unto the sea, which hath requit it,
Him, and his innocent child, for which foul deed
The pow'rs, delaying, not forgetting, have
Incensed the seas and shores, yea, all the creatures,
Against your peace. Thee of thy son, Alonso,   75
They have bereft, and do pronounce by me
Ling'ring perdition, worse than any death
Can be at once, shall step by step attend
You and your ways, whose wraths to guard you from —
Which here, in this most desolate isle, else falls 80
Upon your heads — is nothing but heart's sorrow,
And a clear life ensuing.

He vanishes in thunder. Then, to soft music, enter the SHAPES *again, and dance, with mocks and mows, and carry out the table.*

PROSPERO   Bravely the figure of this harpy hast thou
Performed, my Ariel — a grace it had, devouring.
Of my instruction hast thou nothing bated   85
In what thou hadst to say, so, with good life
And observation strange, my meaner ministers
Their several kinds have done. My high charms work,
And these mine enemies are all knit up
In their distractions. They now are in my pow'r,   90
And in these fits I leave them, while I visit
Young Ferdinand, whom they suppose is drowned,
And his and mine loved darling.

Exit

GONZALO   I' th' name of something holy, sir, why stand you
In this strange stare?

ALONSO   O, it is monstrous, monstrous! 95
Methought the billows spoke, and told me of it,
The winds did sing it to me and the thunder,
That deep and dreadful organ-pipe, pronounced
The name of Prosper — it did bass my trespass.
Therefore my son i' th' ooze is bedded, and   100
I'll seek him deeper than e'er plummet sounded,
And with him there lie mudded.

Exit

Act 3, Scene 3

SEBASTIAN   But one fiend at a time,
  I'll fight their legions o'er.

ANTONIO   I'll be thy second.

         Exeunt SEBASTIAN *and* ANTONIO

GONZALO   All three of them are desperate. Their great guilt,
  Like poison given to work a great time after,
  Now gins to bite the spirits. I do beseech you,
  That are of suppler joints, follow them swiftly,
  And hinder them from what this ecstasy
  May now provoke them to.

ADRIAN   Follow, I pray you.
              Exeunt

105

102-103 'I'll fight them one devil at a time.'

104-109 'Their guilty feelings from all those years ago have started to sink in. You younger chaps, follow them and make sure they don't do themselves any harm.'

Act 3 — Revision Summary

You're not thinking about skipping these questions now are you? Surely not. Just in case you were, now might be a good time to reveal that this book is enabled with an anti-skipping device. Anyone who thinks they might leave the questions till 'later' or 'can't be bothered' will be permanently bonded with molecules closely reproducing the stench of cheese and onion crisps. Nobody wants to go round with people who smell like that. Be warned. Now answer the questions.

SCENE 1

1) Ferdinand says there's something that makes all the work he's got to do for Prospero bearable. What is it?

2) Why does Miranda say it's safe to take a break?

3) Do Ferdinand and Miranda know Prospero's watching them?

4) Why doesn't Miranda know whether she's pretty or not?

5) Explain (in your own words) what Ferdinand means when he says, "I am, in my condition, / A prince, Miranda. I do think, a king — / I would not so".

6) Miranda and Ferdinand agree to get married. Who's first to suggest it, Miranda or Ferdinand?

7) What is Prospero's reaction when he sees Miranda and Ferdinand agree to get hitched?

SCENE 2

8) What does Stephano mean when he says "when the butt is out we will drink water, not a drop before"?

9) Who calls Caliban "servant-monster"?

10) Who calls Caliban "man-monster"?

11) Who does Caliban say is "not valiant"?

12) Explain how Ariel tries to start a fight between Trinculo and the others.

13) Describe Caliban's plan to do away with Prospero.

14) Who does Caliban say will make a good wife for Stephano?

15) Who plays the tune after Stephano sings it wrongly?

16) Is Caliban afraid of the music? Write down the words he says that tell you this.

17) Where do Trinculo, Caliban and Stephano go at the end of the scene?

SCENE 3

18) Which two people say they're tired at the beginning of this scene? Why are they tired?

19) Are Antonio and Sebastian still planning to kill Alonso?

20) Why does Sebastian say he now believes in unicorns and the phoenix?

21) Who convinces Alonso that it's OK to eat the food the spirits leave behind?

22) What shape does Ariel take when he makes the food disappear?

23) Who are the "three men of sin" Ariel is talking to in his long speech?

24) What does Ariel say their punishment is?

25) Is Prospero pleased with the effect Ariel's appearance has on the others?

26) Did Gonzalo see Ariel?

27) What do Sebastian and Antonio go off to do at the end of the scene?

ACT 4 SCENE 1
Before Prospero's cell

Enter PROSPERO, FERDINAND and MIRANDA

PROSPERO   If I have too austerely punished you,
Your compensation makes amends, for I
Have given you here a third of mine own life,
Or that for which I live, who once again
I tender to thy hand. All thy vexations   5
Were but my trials of thy love, and thou
Hast strangely stood the test. Here, afore heaven,
I ratify this my rich gift. O Ferdinand!
Do not smile at me that I boast her off,
For thou shalt find she will outstrip all praise,   10
And make it halt behind her.

1-8 'I know I've been hard on you but I'm making up for it now. I'm handing over a third of my life, the thing that keeps me going. I was testing how much you love her and you've passed. Now, by heaven, she's all yours.'

9-11 'Don't smile when I boast about her. You'll find that she deserves more praise than you can give her.'

FERDINAND   I do believe it
Against an oracle.

oracle = priest or priestess who passes on messages from the gods

PROSPERO   Then, as my gift, and thine own acquisition
Wort'hily purchased, take my daughter. But
If thou dost break her virgin-knot before   15
All sanctimonious ceremonies may
With full and holy rite be minist'red,
No sweet aspersion shall the heavens let fall
To make this contract grow, but barren hate,
Sour-eyed disdain, and discord, shall bestrew   20
The union of your bed with weeds so loathly
That you shall hate it both. Therefore take heed,
As Hymen's lamps shall light you.

14-22 'If you sleep with her before the wedding ceremony, the heavens will curse your marriage and fill it with hate, disrespect and disagreements.'

Hymen's lamps = lamps lit at a Roman wedding in honour of the marriage goddess Hymen

fair issue = lovely babies

FERDINAND   As I hope
For quiet days, fair issue, and long life,
With such love as 'tis now, the murkiest den,   25
The most opportune place, the strong'st suggestion
Our worser genius can, shall never melt
Mine honour into lust, to take away
The edge of that day's celebration,
When I shall think or Phoebus' steeds are foundered 30
Or Night kept chained below.

25-29 'I won't sleep with her, no matter how tempted I am. It would take away the joy of the wedding day'

Phoebus' steeds = horses who pull the Sun god Phoebus' chariot through the sky

foundered = crashed. Ferdinand means he'll be so impatient for night to come, it'll feel like time has stopped

PROSPERO   Fairly spoke.
Sit, then, and talk with her, she is thine own.
What, Ariel! My industrious servant, Ariel!

Enter ARIEL

ARIEL What would my potent master? Here I am.

PROSPERO   Thou and thy meaner fellows your last service 35
Did worthily perform, and I must use you
In such another trick. Go bring the rabble,
O'er whom I give thee pow'r, here to this place.
Incite them to quick motion, for I must
Bestow upon the eyes of this young couple   40
Some vanity of mine art — it is my promise,
And they expect it from me.

thy meaner fellows = the other spirits

37-41 'Go and get the other spirits who I've put in your power. Tell them to hurry up. I want to put on a show for the young couple'

ARIEL   Presently?

presently = now

PROSPERO   Ay, with a twink.

44 'Yes, in the twinkling of an eye.'

with mop and mow = *making cheeky faces*

ARIEL   Before you can say 'come' and 'go,'
　　　And breathe twice, and cry 'so, so,'   45
　　　Each one, tripping on his toe,
　　　Will be here with mop and mow.
　　　Do you love me, master? No?

PROSPERO   Dearly, my delicate Ariel. Do not approach
　　　Till thou dost hear me call.

50 *'All right! I understand.'* →

ARIEL   Well! I conceive.   50

Exit

51-54 *'Make sure you keep your promises. Don't let your loving feelings get the better of you. Swearing strong oaths can make you all the more passionate. Hold off, or you'll break your vow!'*

PROSPERO   Look thou be true. Do not give dalliance
　　　Too much the rein. The strongest oaths are straw
　　　To th' fire i' th' blood. Be more abstemious,
　　　Or else good night your vow!

55-56 *'My heart is pure and controls my passion.'* People believed that feelings of love came from the heart, and that passion and desire came from the liver.

FERDINAND   I warrant you, sir,
　　　The white cold virgin snow upon my heart   55
　　　Abates the ardour of my liver.

57-58 *'better to bring an extra spirit for the show than have one too few'* →

PROSPERO   Well!
　　　Now come, my Ariel, bring a corollary,
　　　Rather than want a spirit. Appear, and pertly.
　　　No tongue! All eyes! Be silent.

Soft music. Enter IRIS.

Ceres = *Greek goddess of harvest and fertility*

60-74 *'Ceres, generous lady, I am a rainbow, a messenger for the Queen of the sky. She asks you to leave your rich fields of wheat, rye, barley, vetch, oats and peas; your grassy mountains and meadows, where the sheep graze; the banks topped with tidy hedges, which rainy April covers in flowers to make garlands for nymphs; your shady groves of broom where rejected lovers go to mope; your neat vineyards; and the barren rocky seashore. Come and join her here for some fun.'*

IRIS   Ceres, most bounteous lady, thy rich leas   60
　　　Of wheat, rye, barley, vetches, oats, and pease,
　　　Thy turfy mountains, where live nibbling sheep,
　　　And flat meads thatched with stover, them to keep,
　　　Thy banks with pioned and twilled brims,
　　　Which spongy April at thy hest betrims,   65
　　　To make cold nymphs chaste crowns, and thy broom groves,
　　　Whose shadow the dismissed bachelor loves,
　　　Being lass-lorn, thy pole-clipt vineyard,
　　　And thy sea-marge, sterile and rocky hard,
　　　Where thou thyself dost air: the Queen o' th' sky,   70
　　　Whose wat'ry arch and messenger am I,
　　　Bids thee leave these, and with her sovereign grace,
　　　Here on this grass-plot, in this very place,

74, stage direction, 77 Juno was Queen of the Roman gods, married to Jupiter, and "Queen of the sky". She travelled around in a carriage drawn by peacocks. Iris, the rainbow, was her messenger.

　　　To come and sport. Her peacocks fly amain.

JUNO *descends*

　　　Approach, rich Ceres, her to entertain.   75

Enter CERES

saffron = *deep yellow*

diffusest = *sprinkle*

CERES   Hail, many-coloured messenger, that ne'er
　　　Dost disobey the wife of Jupiter,
　　　Who, with thy saffron wings, upon my flow'rs
　　　Diffusest honey drops, refreshing show'rs,
　　　And with each end of thy blue bow dost crown   80

81 *'my wooded acres and my open grassy hills'* →

　　　My bosky acres and my unshrubbed down,
　　　Rich scarf to my proud earth — why hath thy Queen
　　　Summoned me hither to this short-grassed green?

IRIS   A contract of true love to celebrate,

84-86 *'To celebrate a vow of true love and to give the blessed lovers a gift.'* →

　　　And some donation freely to estate   85
　　　On the blest lovers.

Venus, her son = *goddess of love, her son Cupid*

CERES   Tell me, heavenly bow,
　　　If Venus or her son, as thou dost know,

Act 4, Scene 1

Do now attend the Queen? Since they did plot
The means that dusky Dis my daughter got,
Her and her blind boy's scandaled company   90
I have forsworn.
IRIS   Of her society
Be not afraid. I met her Deity
Cutting the clouds towards Paphos, and her son
Dove-drawn with her. Here thought they to have done
Some wanton charm upon this man and maid,   95
Whose vows are that no bed-right shall be paid
Till Hymen's torch be lighted, but in vain.
Mars's hot minion is returned again,
Her waspish-headed son has broke his arrows,
Swears he will shoot no more, but play with sparrows, 100
And be a boy right out.
CERES   Highest Queen of State,
Great Juno, comes — I know her by her gait.
JUNO   How does my bounteous sister? Go with me
To bless this twain, that they may prosperous be,
And honoured in their issue.   105
                    They sing:
JUNO   Honour, riches, marriage-blessing,
Long continuance, and increasing,
Hourly joys be still upon you!
Juno sings her blessings on you.
CERES   Earth's increase, foison plenty,   110
Barns and garners never empty;
Vines with clust'ring bunches growing,
Plants with goodly burden bowing,
Spring come to you at the farthest,
In the very end of harvest!   115
Scarcity and want shall shun you,
Ceres' blessing so is on you.
FERDINAND   This is a most majestic vision, and
Harmonious charmingly. May I be bold
To think these spirits?
PROSPERO   Spirits, which by mine art   120
I have from their confines called to enact
My present fancies.
FERDINAND   Let me live here ever,
So rare a wond'red father and a wise
Makes this place Paradise.
  JUNO and CERES whisper, and send IRIS on employment
PROSPERO   Sweet now, silence.
Juno and Ceres whisper seriously.   125
There's something else to do — hush, and be mute,
Or else our spell is marred.
IRIS   You nymphs, called Naiads, of the windring brooks,
With your sedged crowns and ever harmless looks,
Leave your crisp channels, and on this green land   130
Answer your summons. Juno does command.

Dis = another name for Pluto, King of the Underworld

86-91 'Do you know if Venus and Cupid are with the Queen? Ever since they helped the King of the Underworld capture my daughter I've refused to have anything to do with them.'

91-97 'Don't worry, she won't be here. I met her and Cupid flying towards her island, Paphos. She was hoping to get this man and woman into bed, but they're not doing anything of the sort until they've had a proper wedding.'

98-101 'Mars' hot lover (Venus) has gone. Her spoilt son (Cupid) has broken his arrows and swears he will give up shooting, and play with sparrows like any other boy.'

twain = couple

105 'have children who are a credit to them'

foison = riches
garners = grain-stores

116-117 'You will never go short or want for anything — this is my blessing on you.'

118-120 'This is really lovely. Can I assume these are spirits?'

120-122 'That's right. I've called them up with my magic arts to act out my ideas.'

122-124 'I'd like to live here for ever. Having such a wise and extraordinary father makes the place a Paradise.'

on employment = to do a chore

marred = spoiled
nymphs, called Naiads = water-spirits
sedged crowns = garlands made from rushes

Act 4, Scene 1

temperate = *sweet-tempered*

sicklemen = *harvesters*

137-138 *'come and do a country dance with the nymphs'*

properly habited = *in traditional country clothing*

confederates = *allies*

143-144 *'Prospero's in a terrible mood.'*

148-158 *'Show's over. As I said at the beginning, the actors were all spirits and they've vanished into thin air. The world and everything in it will go the same way one day, dissolve away, just like this shadowy performance. We're no more lasting than dreams — our short lives end in death.'*

infirmity = *weakness*

161-163 *'If you like, go and have a rest in my cave. I'm going for a little walk to calm myself down.'*

167-169 *'I was going to remind you when I brought the Ceres-spirit, but I didn't want to make you cross.'*

varlets = *scumbags*

valour = *bravery*

smote = *bashed at*

Come, temperate nymphs, and help to celebrate
A contract of true love — be not too late.

Enter certain NYMPHS

You sun-burnt sicklemen, of August weary,
Come hither from the furrow, and be merry.   135
Make holiday, your rye-straw hats put on,
And these fresh nymphs encounter every one
In country footing.

Enter certain REAPERS, *properly habited. They join with the*
NYMPHS *in a graceful dance, towards the end whereof*
PROSPERO *starts suddenly, and speaks, after which, to a*
strange, hollow, and confused noise, they heavily vanish.

PROSPERO *(aside)* I had forgot that foul conspiracy
Of the beast Caliban and his confederates   140
Against my life. The minute of their plot
Is almost come. *(to the* SPIRITS*)* Well done! Avoid —
                                            no more! *(the* SPIRITS *depart)*

FERDINAND This is strange. Your father's in some passion
That works him strongly.

MIRANDA   Never till this day
Saw I him touched with anger so distempered.   145

PROSPERO You do look, my son, in a moved sort,
As if you were dismayed. Be cheerful, sir.
Our revels now are ended. These our actors,
As I foretold you, were all spirits, and
Are melted into air, into thin air,   150
And, like the baseless fabric of this vision,
The cloud-capped towers, the gorgeous palaces,
The solemn temples, the great globe itself,
Yea, all which it inherit, shall dissolve,
And, like this insubstantial pageant faded,   155
Leave not a rack behind. We are such stuff
As dreams are made on, and our little life
Is rounded with a sleep. Sir, I am vexed.
Bear with my weakness. My old brain is troubled.
Be not disturbed with my infirmity.   160
If you be pleased, retire into my cell
And there repose. A turn or two I'll walk
To still my beating mind.

FERDINAND, MIRANDA   We wish your peace.

Exeunt

PROSPERO Come, with a thought. I thank thee, Ariel, come.

Enter ARIEL

ARIEL Thy thoughts I cleave to. What's thy pleasure?   165

PROSPERO Spirit, we must prepare to meet with Caliban.

ARIEL Ay, my commander. When I presented Ceres
I thought to have told thee of it, but I feared
Lest I might anger thee.

PROSPERO Say again, where didst thou leave these varlets? 170

ARIEL I told you, sir, they were red-hot with drinking,
So full of valour that they smote the air
For breathing in their faces, beat the ground

Act 4, Scene 1

For kissing of their feet, yet always bending
Towards their project. Then I beat my tabor, 175
At which like unbacked colts they pricked their ears,
Advanced their eyelids, lifted up their noses
As they smelt music, so I charmed their ears,
That calf-like they my lowing followed through
Toothed briers, sharp furzes, pricking gorse and thorns, 180
Which entered their frail shins. At last I left them
I' th' filthy mantled pool beyond your cell,
There dancing up to th' chins, that the foul lake
O'erstunk their feet.

PROSPERO   This was well done, my bird.
Thy shape invisible retain thou still. 185
The trumpery in my house, go bring it hither
For stale to catch these thieves.

ARIEL   I go, I go.

Exit

PROSPERO A devil, a born devil, on whose nature
Nurture can never stick, on whom my pains,
Humanely taken, all, all lost, quite lost, 190
And as with age his body uglier grows,
So his mind cankers. I will plague them all,
Even to roaring.

Re-enter ARIEL, loaden with glistering apparel etc.

Come, hang them on this line.

PROSPERO and ARIEL remain, invisible
Enter CALIBAN, STEPHANO and TRINCULO, all wet

CALIBAN Pray you, tread softly, that the blind mole may not
Hear a foot fall — we now are near his cell. 195

STEPHANO Monster, your fairy, which you say is a
harmless fairy, has done little better than played the Jack
with us.

TRINCULO Monster, I do smell all horse-piss at which my
nose is in great indignation. 200

STEPHANO So is mine. Do you hear, monster? If I should
take a displeasure against you, look you —

TRINCULO Thou wert but a lost monster.

CALIBAN Good my lord, give me thy favour still.
Be patient, for the prize I'll bring thee to 205
Shall hoodwink this mischance. Therefore speak softly.
All's hushed as midnight yet.

TRINCULO Ay, but to lose our bottles in the pool!

STEPHANO There is not only disgrace and dishonour in
that, monster, but an infinite loss. 210

TRINCULO That's more to me than my wetting, yet this is
your harmless fairy, monster.

STEPHANO I will fetch off my bottle, though I be o'er ears
for my labour.

CALIBAN Prithee, my king, be quiet. Seest thou here, 215
This is the mouth o' th' cell. No noise, and enter.

174-175 'But all the while they were working towards their plan of attacking you.'

tabor = drum

unbacked colts = untamed young horses

178-184 'I used my music so that they followed me like calves following their mother's mooing, through prickling plants, all the way to the cesspool behind your cell. I left them there up to their chins in it. The pond smells even worse than their feet.'

185-187 'Stay invisible for now. Go and get all the shiny bits and pieces from the house and bring them here. We'll use them as bait to catch the thieves.'

188-193 'Caliban's a devil. There's no training that can overcome his evil nature. I made a real effort with him but it was a waste of time. The older and uglier he gets the more twisted his mind gets. I'll make them suffer — I'll make them roar with pain.'

194-195 'Walk quietly — so quietly that not even a mole can hear your footsteps.'

196-198 'You said that spirit Ariel was harmless, but he's made fools out of us.'

204-206 'Don't be cross my lord. Be patient. This little accident is nothing compared to being king of the island.'

213-214 'I'm going back for my bottle even if I have to go in over my ears.'

215-216 'Please be quiet, my king. Look, here's the mouth of Prospero's cave.'

Act 4, Scene 1

217-219 'Do that bit of business to make the island yours forever, and me your foot-licker for ever.'

frippery = second-hand clothes shop

put off = take off

230-231 'I wish Trinculo would die of a nasty illness! Why are you getting so excited about a load of old rubbish?'

jerkin = leather jacket

236-237 'The line' is what sailors called the Equator. Sailors crossing 'the line' for the first time had their heads shaved in a jolly on-board ritual.

238 'like true craftsmen'. Carpenters use a line and a level to keep their edges straight.

242-243 'a top gag'

lime = sticky glue

246 'I'm having nothing to do with this. It's a waste of time.'

249-251 'Give us a hand, monster. Carry this to where my wine barrel is, or I'll throw you out of my kingdom.'

divers = various

charge = order

convulsions = fits

sinews = muscles

pard = leopard

Do that good mischief which may make this island
Thine own for ever, and I, thy Caliban,
For aye thy foot-licker.

STEPHANO   Give me thy hand. I do begin to have bloody thoughts.   22'

TRINCULO   O King Stephano! O peer! O worthy Stephano! Look what a wardrobe here is for thee!

CALIBAN   Let it alone, thou fool, it is but trash.

TRINCULO   O, ho, monster, we know what belongs to a frippery. O King Stephano!   225

STEPHANO   Put off that gown, Trinculo. By this hand, I'll have that gown.

TRINCULO   Thy Grace shall have it.

CALIBAN   The dropsy drown this fool! What do you mean   230
To dote thus on such luggage? Let 't alone,
And do the murder first. If he awake,
From toe to crown he'll fill our skins with pinches,
Make us strange stuff.

STEPHANO   Be you quiet, monster. Mistress line, is not this   235
my jerkin? Now is the jerkin under the line. Now, jerkin,
you are like to lose your hair, and prove a bald jerkin.

TRINCULO   Do, do. We steal by line and level, an't like your Grace.

STEPHANO   I thank thee for that jest — here's a garment   240
for't. Wit shall not go unrewarded while I am king of this
country. 'Steal by line and level' is an excellent pass of
pate — there's another garment for't.

TRINCULO   Monster, come, put some lime upon your
fingers, and away with the rest.   245

CALIBAN   I will have none on't. We shall lose our time,
And all be turned to barnacles, or to apes
With foreheads villainous low.

STEPHANO   Monster, lay-to your fingers — help to bear this
away where my hogshead of wine is, or I'll turn you out   250
of my kingdom. Go to, carry this.

TRINCULO   And this.

STEPHANO   Ay, and this.

A noise of hunters heard. Enter divers SPIRITS,
in shape of dogs and hounds, hunting them about.
PROSPERO and ARIEL setting them on.

PROSPERO   Hey, Mountain, hey!

ARIEL   Silver! There it goes, Silver!   255

PROSPERO   Fury, Fury! There, Tyrant, there! Hark, hark!

CALIBAN, STEPHANO *and* TRINCULO *are driven out*

Go charge my goblins that they grind their joints
With dry convulsions, shorten up their sinews
With aged cramps, and more pinch-spotted make them
Than pard or cat o' mountain.

ARIEL   Hark, they roar.   260

PROSPERO   Let them be hunted soundly. At this hour
               Lies at my mercy all mine enemies.
               Shortly shall all my labours end, and thou
               Shalt have the air at freedom. For a little
               Follow, and do me service.   265
                                    Exeunt

261-265 *'Right now all my enemies are at my mercy. Soon all my trouble will be over, and I'll set you free. Just follow my orders for a little while longer.'*

Act 4, Scene 1

Act 4 — Revision Summary

Pause. Reflect. Never in the history of revision summaries has so much perfection graced a sheet of paper. Look below and you'll be privileged to experience almost two dozen hand-crafted questions, each brimming with care, wisdom, letters and punctuation. Take the time to answer each of them and we believe you'll find it an even more rewarding experience than it was for our trolls to forge them in our Icelandic revision summary foundry, powered with the heat of ancient volcanoes.

SCENE 1

1) Prospero tells Ferdinand he can marry Miranda — but what is he not allowed to do before they get married?

2) Is Ferdinand happy to go along with this?

3) What does "with a twink" mean?

4) What does Iris look like?

5) What's Iris's job?

6) Who arrives in a carriage pulled by peacocks?

7) Who does Iris call to join them?

8) Why doesn't Ceres like Venus?

9) What's the overall message from the goddesses to Miranda and Ferdinand?

10) What do the Naiads and Reapers do?

11) Prospero interrupts them. Why?

12) How do Ferdinand and Miranda react when Prospero stops the show?

13) What does Prospero suggest the young people do?

14) Why didn't Ariel remind Prospero about Caliban?

15) Where did Ariel lead Stephano, Trinculo and Caliban?

16) What does Trinculo smell of?

17) What has Stephano lost?

18) What do the three trouble-makers find at the mouth of Prospero's cave?

19) Caliban thinks the other two are wasting time. What are they doing?

20) Ariel and Prospero return with spirits in the shape of hunting dogs. Write down three of the dogs' names.

21) What other punishments does Prospero order?

22) What does Prospero mean when he says "At this hour / Lies at my mercy all mine enemies"?

ACT 5 SCENE 1
Before Prospero's cell

Enter PROSPERO *in his magic robes, and* ARIEL

Ariel brings Alonso and the other lords to Prospero. Prospero shouts at them for a while and then forgives them. He reveals that Ferdinand is still alive and is going to marry Miranda.

PROSPERO   Now does my project gather to a head.
　My charms crack not, my spirits obey, and time
　Goes upright with his carriage. How's the day?

1-3 'My plans are working out brilliantly. The magic's working, the spirits are behaving and everything's on schedule. What's the time?'

ARIEL   On the sixth hour, at which time, my lord,
　You said our work should cease.

PROSPERO　　　　　　　　　　　I did say so,　　　5
　When first I raised the tempest. Say, my spirit,
　How fares the King and 's followers?

7 'How are the king and his followers doing?'

ARIEL　　　　　　　　　　　　Confined together

7-8 'All detained just as you ordered'
line-grove = small wood of lime trees

　In the same fashion as you gave in charge,
　Just as you left them — all prisoners, sir,
　In the line-grove which weather-fends your cell.　　10
　They cannot budge till your release. The King,
　His brother, and yours, abide all three distracted,

12 'are all a bit mad still'

　And the remainder mourning over them,
　Brim full of sorrow and dismay, but chiefly
　Him you termed, sir, 'the good old lord, Gonzalo'.　　15
　His tears run down his beard, like winter's drops
　From eaves of reeds. Your charm so strongly works 'em
　That if you now beheld them your affections
　Would become tender.

17-19 'Your magic's having such a strong effect on them that if you saw them now it would make you feel really sorry for them.'

PROSPERO　　　　　　　　Dost thou think so, spirit?

ARIEL   Mine would, sir, were I human.

PROSPERO　　　　　　　　　　And mine shall.　　20
　Hast thou, which art but air, a touch, a feeling
　Of their afflictions, and shall not myself,
　One of their kind, that relish all as sharply,
　Passion as they, be kindlier moved than thou art?
　Though with their high wrongs I am struck to th' quick,　　25
　Yet with my nobler reason 'gainst my fury
　Do I take part. The rarer action is
　In virtue than in vengeance. They being penitent,
　The sole drift of my purpose doth extend
　Not a frown further. Go release them, Ariel.　　30
　My charms I'll break, their senses I'll restore,
　And they shall be themselves.

21-30 'You're made of air, and you feel sorry for them, so I should be even more touched. The things they've done to me really upset me but I'll control my anger with reason. Forgiveness is more worthy than revenge. If they're sorry for what they've done now I don't need to be cross any more.'

ARIEL　　　　　　　　　　　　I'll fetch them, sir.

Exit

PROSPERO   *(drawing a magic circle on the ground)*
　Ye elves of hills, brooks, standing lakes, and groves;
　And ye that on the sands with printless foot
　Do chase the ebbing Neptune, and do fly him　　35
　When he comes back; you demi-puppets that
　By moonshine do the green sour ringlets make,
　Whereof the ewe not bites; and you whose pastime
　Is to make midnight mushrooms, that rejoice

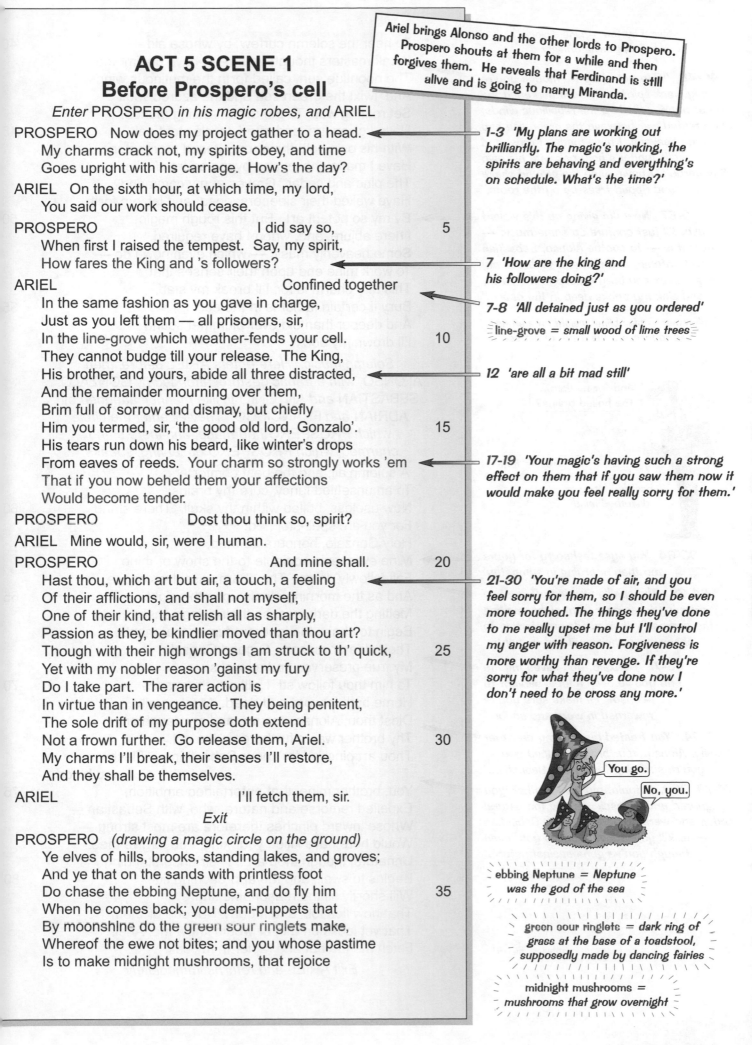

You go.
No, you.

ebbing Neptune = Neptune was the god of the sea

green sour ringlets = dark ring of grass at the base of a toadstool, supposedly made by dancing fairies

midnight mushrooms = mushrooms that grow overnight

Act 5, Scene 1

solemn curfew = *nine o'clock bell, beginning of night*

40-48 *'With your help — though you're only weak spirits — I have darkened the sun at noon, called up the rebellious winds, and created war between the green sea and blue heavens. I have made storms, and split Jupiter's holy oak with his own thunderbolt. I have made the ground shake and ripped trees up by the roots.'*

50-57 *'Now I'm giving up this violent magic. I'll just conjure up some music — there it is — to soothe Alonso, Sebastian and Antonio, and that's it. I'll break my magic stick and bury it deep in the earth, and sink my books deep in the ocean.'*

plummet = *plumbline, weight on a string used to measure the depth of the sea*

And for madam...
The boiled brains?

air = *tune*

unsettled fancy = *disturbed mind*

63-64 *'my eyes feel sorry for yours and they're crying in sympathy'*

64-68 *'The spell's wearing off. Just as morning takes over from night, melting the darkness, their minds are starting to chase away their muddled thoughts.'*

68-71 *'Gonzalo, you saved my life and you've been a loyal servant to Alonso! I'll make sure you're rewarded in word and action.'*

71-74 *'You treated me and my daughter cruelly, Alonso. Your brother helped you — you're suffering for it now, Sebastian.'*

74-79 *'You, Antonio, my own brother, you ignored your conscience and the natural order, and were prepared — with Sebastian — to kill your King. I forgive you, even though you've gone against nature.'*

rapier = *sword*

To hear the solemn curfew; by whose aid —   40
Weak masters though ye be — I have bedimmed
The noontide sun, called forth the mutinous winds,
And 'twixt the green sea and the azured vault
Set roaring war. To the dread rattling thunder
Have I given fire, and rifted Jove's stout oak   45
With his own bolt; the strong-based promontory
Have I made shake, and by the spurs plucked up
The pine and cedar. Graves at my command
Have waked their sleepers, oped, and let 'em forth,
By my so potent art. But this rough magic   50
I here abjure, and, when I have required
Some heavenly music — which even now I do —
To work mine end upon their senses that
This airy charm is for, I'll break my staff,
Bury it certain fathoms in the earth,   55
And deeper than did ever plummet sound
I'll drown my book.

   Solemn music. Here enters ARIEL *before, then* ALONSO, *with a frantic gesture, attended by* GONZALO, SEBASTIAN *and* ANTONIO *in like manner, attended by* ADRIAN *and* FRANCISCO. *They all enter the circle which* PROSPERO *had made, and there stand charmed, which* PROSPERO *observing, speaks:*

A solemn air, and the best comforter
To an unsettled fancy, cure thy brains,
Now useless, boiled within thy skull. There stand,   60
For you are spell-stopped.
Holy Gonzalo, honourable man,
Mine eyes, ev'n sociable to the show of thine,
Fall fellowly drops. The charm dissolves apace,
And as the morning steals upon the night,   65
Melting the darkness, so their rising senses
Begin to chase the ignorant fumes that mantle
Their clearer reason. O good Gonzalo,
My true preserver, and a loyal sir
To him thou follow'st! I will pay thy graces   70
Home both in word and deed. Most cruelly
Didst thou, Alonso, use me and my daughter.
Thy brother was a furtherer in the act. —
Thou art pinched for't now, Sebastian. — Flesh
               and blood,
You, brother mine, that entertained ambition,   75
Expelled remorse and nature, who, with Sebastian —
Whose inward pinches therefore are most strong —
Would here have killed your king, I do forgive thee,
Unnatural though thou art. Their understanding
Begins to swell, and the approaching tide   80
Will shortly fill the reasonable shore
That now lies foul and muddy. Not one of them
That yet looks on me, or would know me. Ariel,
Fetch me the hat and rapier in my cell.

    Exit ARIEL *and returns immediately*

I will discase me, and myself present   85
As I was sometime Milan. Quickly, spirit
Thou shalt ere long be free.

ARIEL *(sings and helps to attire him)*
Where the bee sucks, there suck I;
In a cowslip's bell I lie;
There I couch when owls do cry.   90
On the bat's back I do fly
After summer merrily.
Merrily, merrily shall I live now
Under the blossom that hangs on the bough.

PROSPERO Why, that's my dainty Ariel! I shall miss thee;   95
But yet thou shalt have freedom. So, so, so.
To the King's ship, invisible as thou art.
There shalt thou find the mariners asleep
Under the hatches. The master and the boatswain
Being awake, enforce them to this place,   100
And presently, I prithee.

ARIEL I drink the air before me, and return
Or ere your pulse twice beat.

Exit

GONZALO All torment, trouble, wonder and amazement,
Inhabits here. Some heavenly power guide us   105
Out of this fearful country!

PROSPERO   Behold, Sir King,
The wronged Duke of Milan, Prospero.
For more assurance that a living prince
Does now speak to thee, I embrace thy body,
And to thee and thy company I bid   110
A hearty welcome.

ALONSO   Whe'er thou be'st he or no,
Or some enchanted trifle to abuse me,
As late I have been, I not know. Thy pulse
Beats, as of flesh and blood, and, since I saw thee,
Th' affliction of my mind amends, with which,   115
I fear, a madness held me. This must crave —
An if this be at all — a most strange story.
Thy dukedom I resign, and do entreat
Thou pardon me my wrongs. But how should Prospero
Be living and be here?

PROSPERO   First, noble friend,   120
Let me embrace thine age, whose honour cannot
Be measured or confined.

GONZALO   Whether this be
Or be not, I'll not swear.

PROSPERO   You do yet taste
Some subtleties o' th' isle, that will not let you
Believe things certain. Welcome, my friends all!   125
(aside to SEBASTIAN and ANTONIO)
But you, my brace of lords, were I so minded,
I here could pluck his Highness' frown upon you,
And justify you traitors — at this time

85-86 *'I'll get changed into the kind of thing I wore when I was Duke of Milan.'*

under the hatches = below decks

99-101 *'When you've woken the master and boatswain, bring them here, and quickly please.'*

WAY OUT

Behold = look

108-109 *'I'll hug you to prove I'm real'*

111-113 *'I don't know whether you're him or not, or another magic trick.'*

114-116 *'since I've seen you the sickness in my mind has lifted. I think it was making me mad.*

116-120 *'There must be a strange explanation for this. Have your dukedom back and pardon me. How come you're still alive and living here?'*

120-122 *'First, let me hug my worthy old friend Gonzalo.'*

123-125 *'You're still under the influence of the magic of the island so you can't be sure of anything.'*

126-129 *'I could get you two into serious trouble with Alonso and prove you're traitors if I felt like it. But I won't do it now.'*

Act 5, Scene 1

I will tell no tales.

SEBASTIAN *(aside)* The devil speaks in him.

PROSPERO   No.

129 *'The devil's speaking through him — it's not true.'*

For you, most wicked sir, whom to call brother   130
Would even infect my mouth, I do forgive
Thy rankest fault — all of them — and require
My dukedom of thee, which perforce I know
Thou must restore.

130-134 *'As for you, it disgusts me to call you brother, but I forgive you. Now give me my dukedom back — you've got to.'*

ALONSO   If thou be'st Prospero,
Give us particulars of thy preservation,   135
How thou hast met us here, whom three hours since
Were wrecked upon this shore, where I have lost —
How sharp the point of this remembrance is! —
My dear son Ferdinand.

134-139 *'If you really are Prospero, explain how you survived and tell us how we've ended up here. Just three hours ago we were shipwrecked, and I lost my lovely Ferdinand.'*

PROSPERO.   I am woe for't, sir.

woe = sorry

ALONSO Irreparable is the loss, and patience   140
Says it is past her cure.

140-141 *'There's no consolation for it and I don't think time will make it feel any better.'*

PROSPERO   I rather think
You have not sought her help, of whose soft grace
For the like loss I have her sovereign aid,
And rest myself content.

141-144 *'I think you've got to be patient. Patience has helped me with my loss.'*

ALONSO   You the like loss?

PROSPERO As great to me as late, and, supportable   145
To make the dear loss, have I means much weaker
Than you may call to comfort you, for I
Have lost my daughter.

145-147 *'I've lost as much and as recently as you. It's even harder for me to cope with my loss'*

ALONSO   A daughter!
O heavens, that they were living both in Naples,
The King and Queen there! That they were, I wish   150
Myself were mudded in that oozy bed
Where my son lies. When did you lose your daughter?

151 *'lying drowned in the mud at the bottom of the sea'*

PROSPERO In this last tempest. I perceive these lords
At this encounter do so much admire
That they devour their reason, and scarce think   155
Their eyes do offices of truth, their words
Are natural breath, but, howsoe'er you have
Been jostled from your senses, know for certain
That I am Prospero, and that very duke
Which was thrust forth of Milan, who most strangely   160
Upon this shore, where you were wrecked, was landed
To be the lord on't. No more yet of this,
For 'tis a chronicle of day by day,
Not a relation for a breakfast, nor
Befitting this first meeting. Welcome, sir —   165
This cell's my court. Here have I few attendants,
And subjects none abroad. Pray you, look in.
My dukedom since you have given me again,
I will requite you with as good a thing,
At least bring forth a wonder, to content ye   170
As much as me my dukedom.

153-162 *'I can see it's hard for these lords to believe what they're seeing. They think they've gone mad. But however confused you are, it's certain that I am Prospero, the same man who was thrown out of Milan and ended up as lord of this island where you've been wrecked.'*

164 *'not a suitable topic when you're hungry'*

167-171 *'Have a look in my cell. Seeing as you've given me my dukedom back I'll show you something that will please you just as much.'*

discovers = reveals

*Here PROSPERO discovers FERDINAND
and MIRANDA, playing at chess*

MIRANDA   Sweet lord, you play me false.

FERDINAND   No, my dearest love,
  I would not for the world.

MIRANDA   Yes, for a score of kingdoms you should wrangle
  And I would call it fair play.

ALONSO   If this prove   175
  A vision of the island, one dear son
  Shall I twice lose.

SEBASTIAN   A most high miracle!

FERDINAND   Though the seas threaten, they are merciful.
  I have cursed them without cause. *(kneels)*

ALONSO   Now all the blessings
  Of a glad father compass thee about!   180
  Arise, and say how thou cam'st here.

MIRANDA   O, wonder!
  How many goodly creatures are there here!
  How beauteous mankind is! O brave new world
  That has such people in't!

PROSPERO   'Tis new to thee.

ALONSO   What is this maid with whom thou wast at play?   185
  Your eld'st acquaintance cannot be three hours.
  Is she the goddess that hath severed us,
  And brought us thus together?

FERDINAND   Sir, she is mortal,
  But by immortal Providence she's mine.
  I chose her when I could not ask my father   190
  For his advice, nor thought I had one. She
  Is daughter to this famous Duke of Milan,
  Of whom so often I have heard renown
  But never saw before, of whom I have
  Received a second life, and second father   195
  This lady makes him to me.

ALONSO   I am hers.
  But, O, how oddly will it sound that I
  Must ask my child forgiveness!

PROSPERO   There, sir, stop.
  Let us not burden our remembrances with
  A heaviness that's gone.

GONZALO   I have inly wept,   200
  Or should have spoke ere this. Look down, you gods,
  And on this couple drop a blessed crown,
  For it is you that have chalked forth the way
  Which brought us hither.

ALONSO   I say, Amen, Gonzalo!

GONZALO   Was Milan thrust from Milan, that his issue   205
  Should become Kings of Naples? O, rejoice
  Beyond a common joy, and set it down
  With gold on lasting pillars: in one voyage
  Did Claribel her husband find at Tunis;
  And Ferdinand, her brother, found a wife   210
  Where he himself was lost; Prospero his dukedom

you play me false
= you're cheating

174-175 'If you were fighting for twenty kingdoms I'd say that was fair play.'

175-176 'If this turns out to be an illusion I'll have lost Ferdinand twice.'

compass thee about
= surround you

Oooh! You're all so handsome!

What = who

186-188 'You can't have known her for more than three hours. Is she the goddess who separated us and brought us back together?'

immortal Providence = God's good will

198-199 'Let's not upset ourselves by thinking about our past troubles.'

inly = inside me

ere = before

hither = here

205-206 'Was the Duke of Milan thrown out of Milan so his descendants could be Kings of Naples?' Now Prospero's daughter is marrying Alonso's son, their children will be Kings and Queens of Naples.

lasting pillars = stone monuments

Act 5, Scene 1

In a poor isle; and all of us ourselves
When no man was his own.

ALONSO *(to FERDINAND and MIRANDA)*
                              Give me your hands.
Let grief and sorrow still embrace his heart
That doth not wish you joy.

GONZALO   Be it so. Amen!   215

Re-enter ARIEL, with the MASTER and
BOATSWAIN amazedly following

O look, sir! Look, sir! Here is more of us!
I prophesied, if a gallows were on land,
This fellow could not drown. Now, blasphemy,
That swear'st grace o'erboard, not an oath on shore?
Hast thou no mouth by land? What is the news?   220

BOATSWAIN   The best news is that we have safely found
Our King and company. The next, our ship —
Which but three glasses since we gave out split —
Is tight and yare, and bravely rigged, as when
We first put out to sea.   22~

ARIEL *(aside to PROSPERO)* Sir, all this service
Have I done since I went.

PROSPERO *(aside to ARIEL)* My tricksy spirit!

ALONSO   These are not natural events. They strengthen
From strange to stranger. Say, how came you hither?   230

BOATSWAIN   If I did think, sir, I were well awake,
I'd strive to tell you. We were dead of sleep,
And — how, we know not — all clapped under hatches,
Where, but even now, with strange and several noises
Of roaring, shrieking, howling, jingling chains,   235
And more diversity of sounds, all horrible,
We were awaked, straightway at liberty,
Where we, in all our trim, freshly beheld
Our royal, good, and gallant ship, our master
Cap'ring to eye her. On a trice, so please you,   240
Even in a dream, were we divided from them,
And were brought moping hither.

ARIEL *(aside to PROSPERO)*   Was't well done?

PROSPERO *(aside to ARIEL)*
Bravely, my diligence. Thou shalt be free.

ALONSO   This is as strange a maze as e'er men trod,
And there is in this business more than nature   245
Was ever conduct of. Some oracle
Must rectify our knowledge.

PROSPERO   Sir, my liege,
Do not infest your mind with beating on
The strangeness of this business. At picked leisure,
Which shall be shortly, single I'll resolve you,   250
Which to you shall seem probable, of every
These happened accidents, till when, be cheerful
And think of each thing well. *(aside to ARIEL)*
                              Come hither, spirit.

216-218 Gonzalo refers back to what he said in Act 1 Scene 1, that the boatswain is fated to be hanged, so he can't drown.

Ariel brings in the master and the boatswain of Alonso's ship. They're fine but a bit confused.

218-220 *'Now, you blasphemer, don't you swear on shore? Are you tongue-tied on land?'*

222-225 *'Our ship, which three hours ago we thought had split, is just as sound and swift and well-equipped as when we first set out.'*

tricksy = *clever*

231-233 *'If I was properly awake I'd tell you. We were all sound asleep, and shut up below decks — I don't understand how.'*

straightway at liberty = *instantly freed*

Cap'ring to eye her = *jumping for joy to see her*

240-242 *'All at once we were separated from the other sailors and brought here in a kind of dream state.'*

244-247 *'This is a funny old business, and definitely not natural. I think we need an explanation from the gods.'*

248-252 *'Don't stress yourself trying to understand all the odd things that have happened. Soon enough, when we're more relaxed, I'll explain everything properly'*

Set Caliban and his companions free.
Untie the spell.

Exit ARIEL

(to Alonso)   How fares my gracious sir?   255
There are yet missing of your company
Some few odd lads that you remember not.

Re-enter ARIEL, *driving in* CALIBAN, STEPHANO
and TRINCULO, *in their stolen apparel.*

STEPHANO   Every man shift for all the rest, and let no man
take care for himself, for all is but fortune. Coraggio,
bully-monster, coraggio!   260

TRINCULO   If these be true spies which I wear in my head,
here's a goodly sight.

CALIBAN   O Setebos, these be brave spirits indeed!
How fine my master is! I am afraid
He will chastise me.

SEBASTIAN   Ha, ha!   265
What things are these, my lord Antonio?
Will money buy 'em?

ANTONIO   Very like. One of them
Is a plain fish, and no doubt marketable.

PROSPERO   Mark but the badges of these men, my lords,
Then say if they be true. This mis-shapen knave —   270
His mother was a witch, and one so strong
That could control the moon, make flows and ebbs,
And deal in her command without her power.
These three have robbed me, and this demi-devil —
For he's a bastard one — had plotted with them   275
To take my life. Two of these fellows you
Must know and own. This thing of darkness I
Acknowledge mine.

CALIBAN   I shall be pinched to death.

ALONSO   Is not this Stephano, my drunken butler?

SEBASTIAN   He is drunk now — where had he wine?   280

ALONSO   And Trinculo is reeling ripe. Where should they
Find this grand liquor that hath gilded 'em?
How cam'st thou in this pickle?

TRINCULO   I have been in such a pickle since I saw you last
that, I fear me, will never out of my bones. I shall not   285
fear fly-blowing.

SEBASTIAN   Why, how now, Stephano!

STEPHANO   O, touch me not — I am not Stephano, but a
cramp.

PROSPERO   You'd be king o' the isle, sirrah?   290

STEPHANO   I should have been a sore one, then.

ALONSO   *(pointing to* CALIBAN*)* This is as strange a thing
as e'er I looked on.

PROSPERO   He is as disproportioned in his manners
As in his shape. Go, sirrah, to my cell.   295
Take with you your companions. As you look

---

255 'How are you?'

Ariel fetches Stephano, Trinculo and Caliban. They get a ticking off too, and are sent to tidy Prospero's cell for the visitors. Finally, Prospero frees Ariel.

apparel = clothes

258-260 'Everyone help everyone else, and nobody look after himself. It's all just luck. Chin up, brave monster!'

261-262 'If I can believe my eyes, this is a fine sight.'

Setebos = the evil spirit who Caliban's mother worked with

chastise = punish

269-270 'Look at their uniforms and tell me if they're genuine.' Servants like Trinculo and Stephano would have dressed in the house colours of their employer.

271-273 'strong enough to control the moon and change the tides, and do the moon's work without its power'

276-278 'You'll have to take responsibility for two of these fellows. I'm afraid the monster's mine.'

278 Prospero has given Caliban, Stephano and Trinculo cramps and pains to punish them.

reeling ripe = really drunk

284-286 'I've been so soaked in alcohol since I last saw you that I'm afraid I'll never sober up. I won't be infested by flies.' Flies would lay eggs on fresh food, but not on pickled food.

sirrah = young lad

294-297 'His character's as twisted as his body. Go to my cell, Caliban, and take your friends with you. If you want my forgiveness you'd better make it look gorgeous.'

Act 5, Scene 1

To have my pardon, trim it handsomely.

CALIBAN Ay, that I will, and I'll be wise hereafter,
And seek for grace. What a thrice-double ass
Was I to take this drunkard for a god,   300
And worship this dull fool!

PROSPERO   Go to! Away!

ALONSO Hence, and bestow your luggage where you
found it.

SEBASTIAN Or stole it, rather.

Exeunt CALIBAN, STEPHANO *and* TRINCULO

PROSPERO Sir, I invite your Highness and your train   305
To my poor cell, where you shall take your rest
For this one night, which, part of it, I'll waste
With such discourse as, I not doubt, shall make it
Go quick away — the story of my life,
And the particular accidents gone by   310
Since I came to this isle. And in the morn
I'll bring you to your ship, and so to Naples,
Where I have hope to see the nuptial
Of these our dear-beloved solemnized,
And thence retire me to my Milan, where   315
Every third thought shall be my grave.

ALONSO   I long
To hear the story of your life, which must
Take the ear strangely.

PROSPERO   I'll deliver all,
And promise you calm seas, auspicious gales,
And sail so expeditious that shall catch   320
Your royal fleet far off. *(aside to* ARIEL) My Ariel, chick,
That is thy charge. Then to the elements
Be free, and fare thou well!
            (to the others) Please you, draw near.
                    Exeunt

298-299 *'I will, and I'll be sensible from now on and look for your favour.'*

302-303 *'Go away, and put those things back where you found them.'*

train = followers

discourse = conversation

311-315 *'in the morning I'll take you to your ship and we'll go to Naples, where I'd like to see our beloved children married, and from there I'll go back to Milan'*

318-321 *'I'll tell you everything. I also promise you calm seas, favourable wind, and such a speedy journey that you'll catch up with the rest of the royal fleet.'*

321-323 *'Ariel, sweety, that's your job. After that you're free to go. Good luck!'*

EPILOGUE
Spoken by PROSPERO

Now my charms are all o'erthrown,
And what strength I have's mine own,
Which is most faint. Now 'tis true,
I must be here confined by you,
Or sent to Naples. Let me not,   5
Since I have my dukedom got,
And pardoned the deceiver, dwell
In this bare island by your spell,
But release me from my bands
With the help of your good hands.   10
Gentle breath of yours my sails
Must fill, or else my project fails,
Which was to please. Now I want
Spirits to enforce, art to enchant;
And my ending is despair   15
Unless I be relieved by prayer,
Which pierces so that it assaults
Mercy itself, and frees all faults.
As you from crimes would pardoned be,
Let your indulgence set me free.   20

An epilogue is a speech at the end of the play. This one's spoken by Prospero but some of the things he says have double meanings — they could also be the words of the actor addressing the audience.

1 'Now I've lost all my magical powers'

3-5 'It's up to you now, whether I stay trapped here on the island or go back to Naples.'

9-12 This could be meant literally, as in 'carry me away and help my ship go faster by blowing on the sails' or it could mean 'clap and cheer'.

13-18 'I haven't got spirits to command, or magical powers now. My life will end sadly unless prayer can help me. Prayer is powerful enough to win mercy and forgiveness.'

19-20 'Just as you would like to be forgiven for your faults, please be generous and forgive me.'

Ta-ra!

Act 5 — Revision Summary

That's it — you've read the whole play. Whether or not you enjoyed it you may as well answer these questions for a sense of smug completeness. And after that you can reward yourself with some delicious home-baked flapjacks. See below.

SCENE 1

1) What's Prospero wearing at the beginning of the scene?

2) Where are Alonso, Antonio, Sebastian and Gonzalo before Ariel fetches them?

3) How does Ariel feel about the state the lords are in?

4) How does this make Prospero feel?

5) What does Prospero say the "elves of hills, brooks, standing lakes and groves" have helped him do in the past? (CLUE: the answer's buried somewhere in the speech that starts at line 33 and ends at line 57.)

6) What is Prospero going to do with his magic staff and his books?

7) Which characters are led into Prospero's magic circle? Who leads them in?

8) How does the 'solemn air' help them?

9) What makes Prospero cry?

10) Why does Prospero send Ariel to fetch his hat and sword from the cave?

11) What's the next order for Ariel?

12) Why does Prospero hug Alonso?

13) Who does he hug next?

14) Why doesn't he hug Antonio and Sebastian?

15) Prospero says he knows how Alonso feels about losing his son because he's lost his daughter. Alonso thinks he means she's dead. What does Prospero really mean?

16) What are Ferdinand and Miranda doing when Prospero reveals them to the others?

17) Who does Alonso think might be a goddess?

18) What does the boatswain say about the state the ship's in?

19) How much time has passed since the ship seemed to be sinking?

20) Who does Ariel bring in after the boatswain and master?

21) What are they wearing?

22) Who is the 'mis-shapen knave'?

23) Who is 'in a pickle'?

24) Who is a 'cramp'?

25) What does Prospero invite Alonso and the others to do?

26) Who does Prospero call 'chick'?

EPILOGUE

27) What's an epilogue?

28) What are Prospero's 'charms'?

29) What does he say is all up to the audience now?

30) What does he say the 'project' of the play was?

Tempest Flapjacks
75g butter
75g light brown sugar
1 tablespoon golden syrup
175g porridge oats
3 mackerel (optional)

- Preheat the oven to 180°C
- Put the butter, sugar and golden syrup into a saucepan. Stir over a low heat until everything has melted and combined.
- Stir in the porridge oats and mackerel if desired.
- Press the mixture into an oven-proof dish with the back of a spoon.
- Bake for 25 minutes on the middle shelf until evenly golden brown.
- Take out of the oven. Cut into squares while the flapjack's still warm but leave it in the tin to cool.
- Eat as soon as it's not too hot to touch. Or sooner.